# Simple Animals

## A Coloring Book for All Ages

*illustrated by*
Rachel Jones

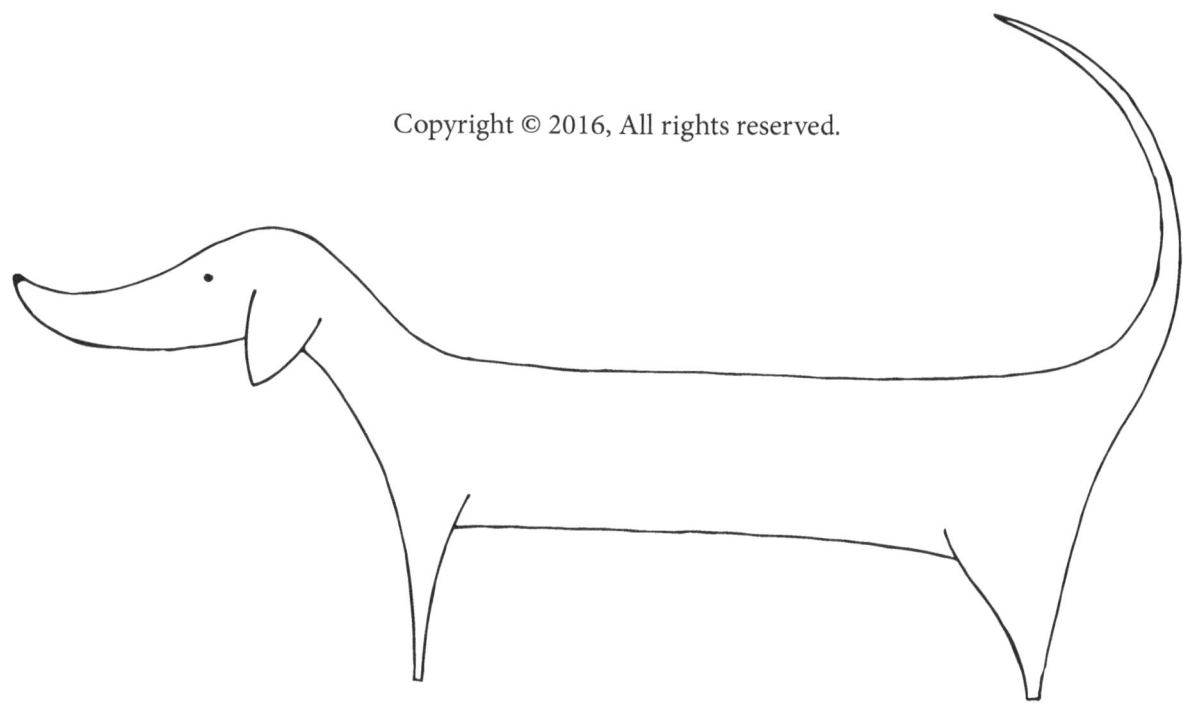

**FREE BONUS PAGES**
Visit: http://racheljonesarts.com/simpleanimals/ to receive a PDF of 5 bonus coloring pages.

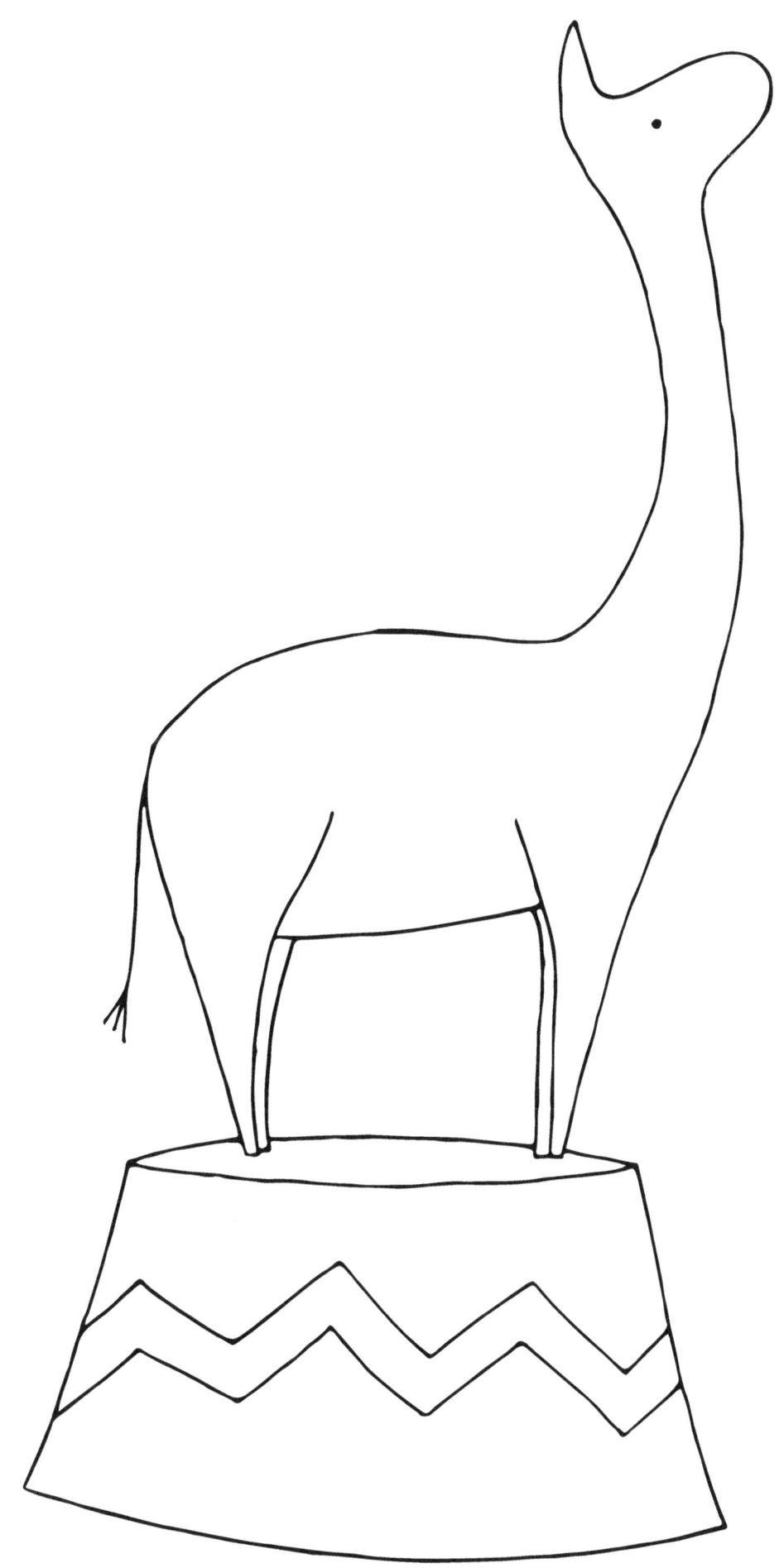

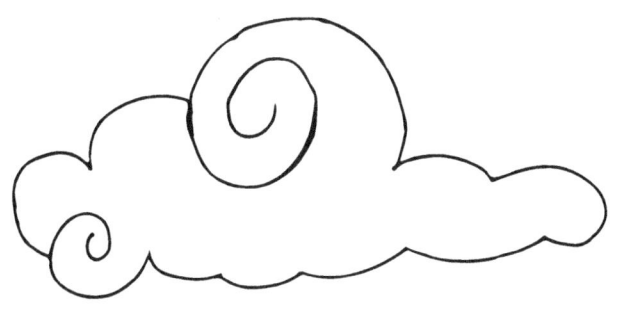

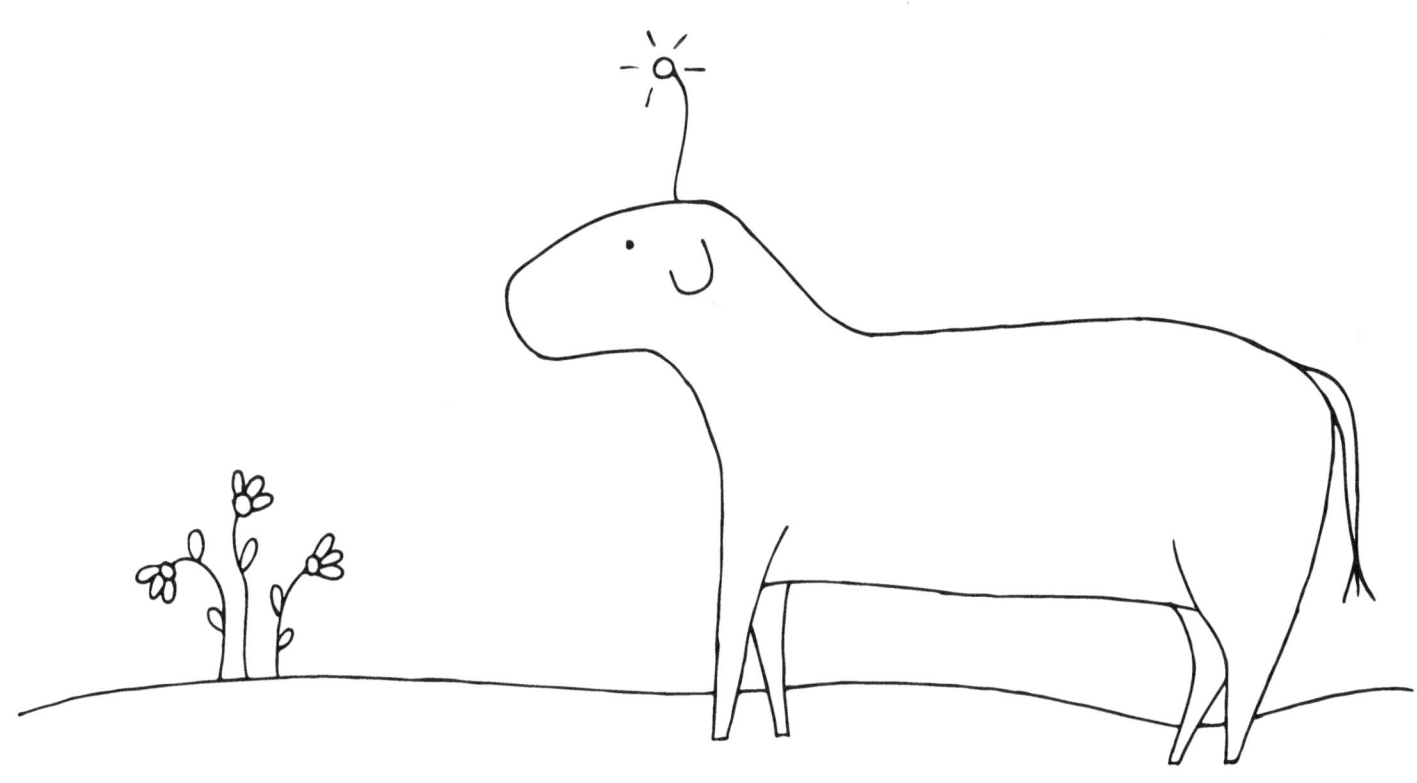

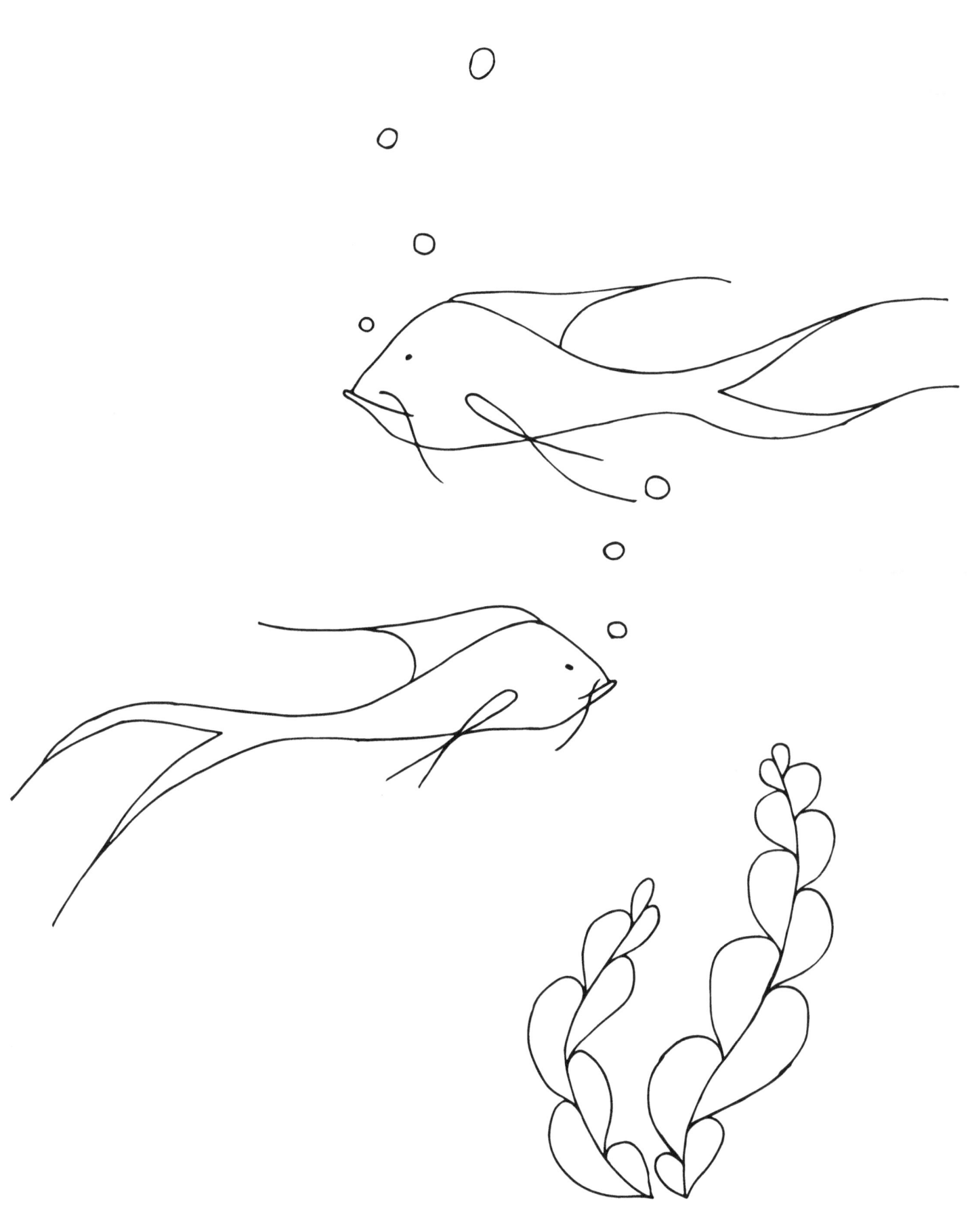

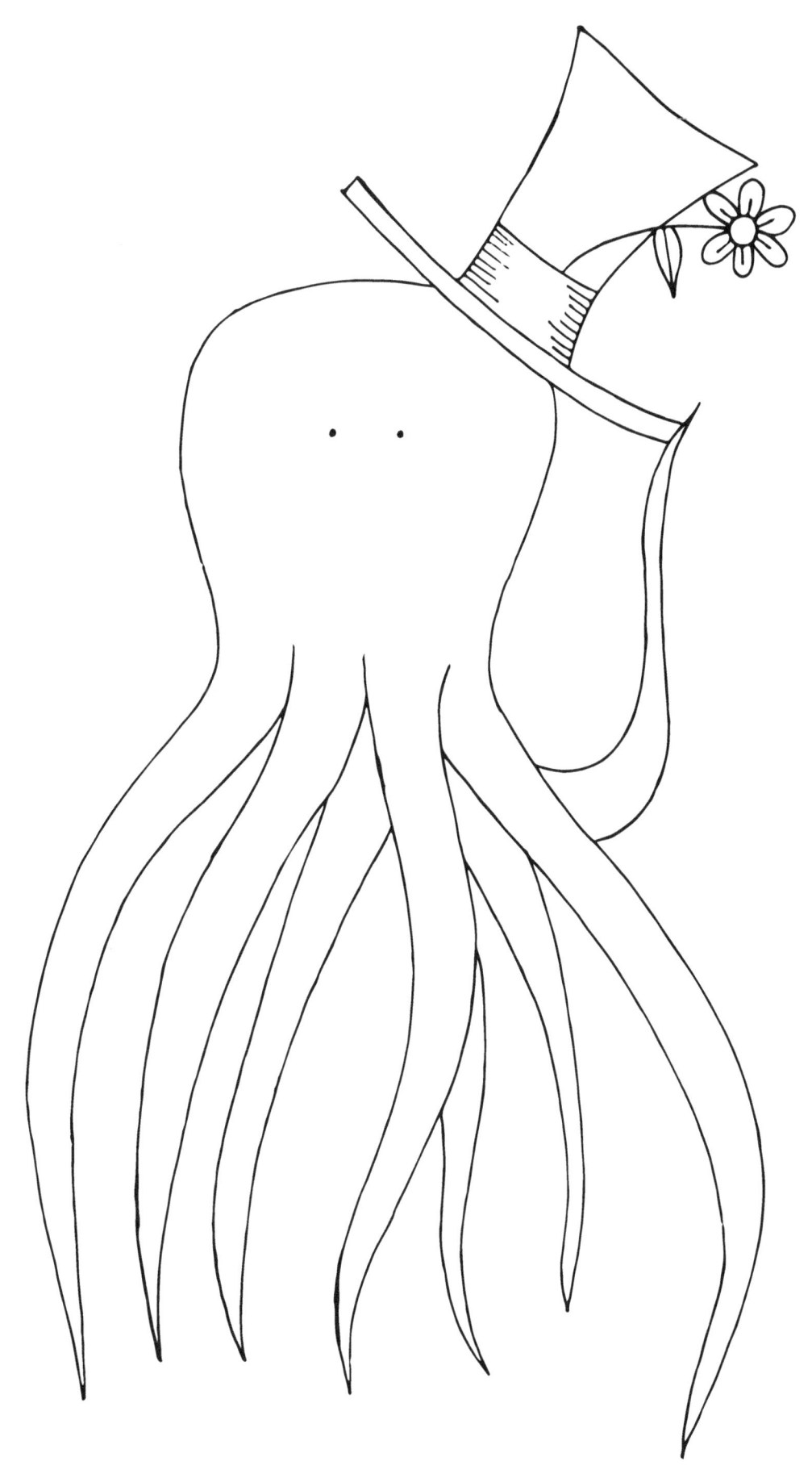

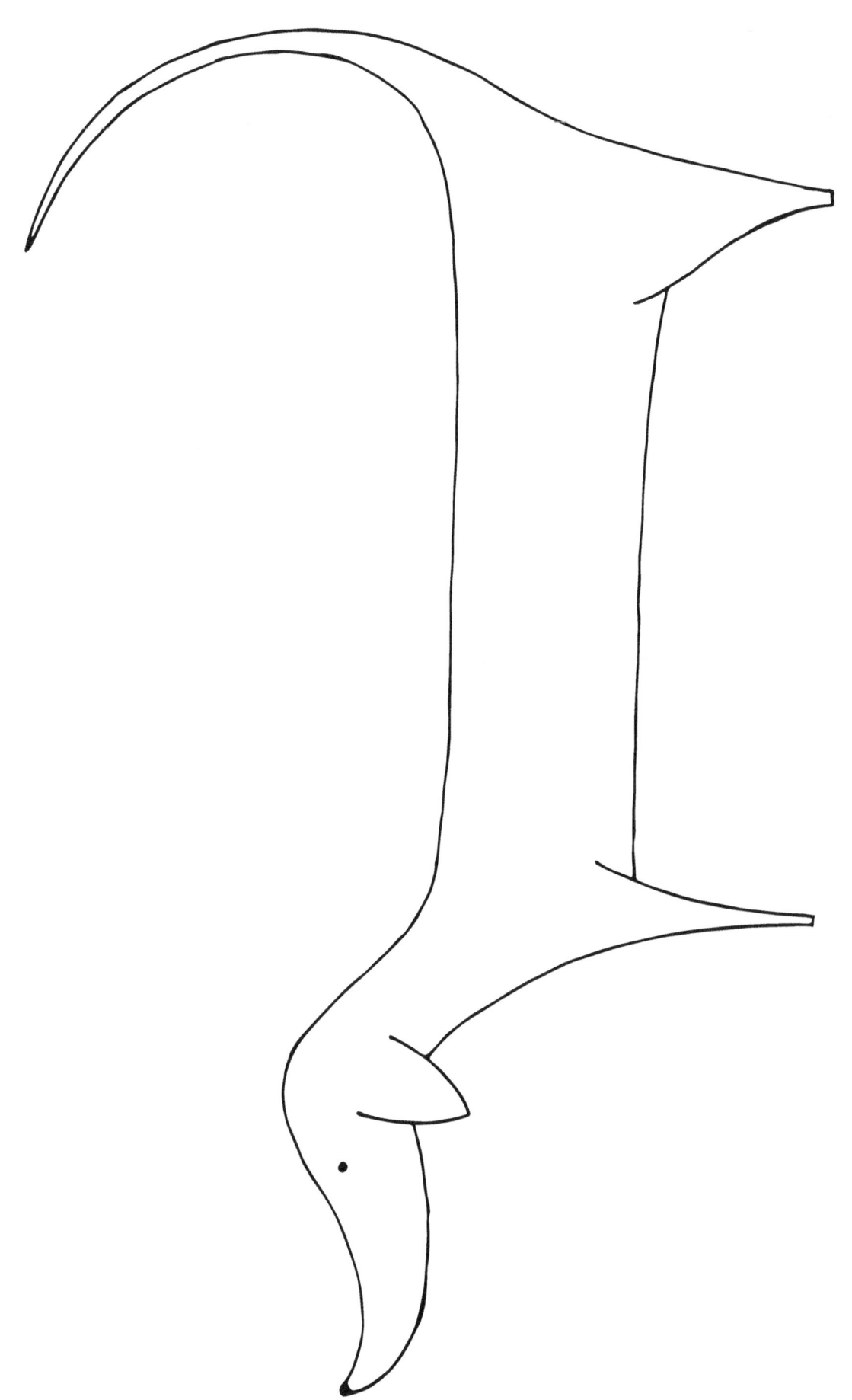

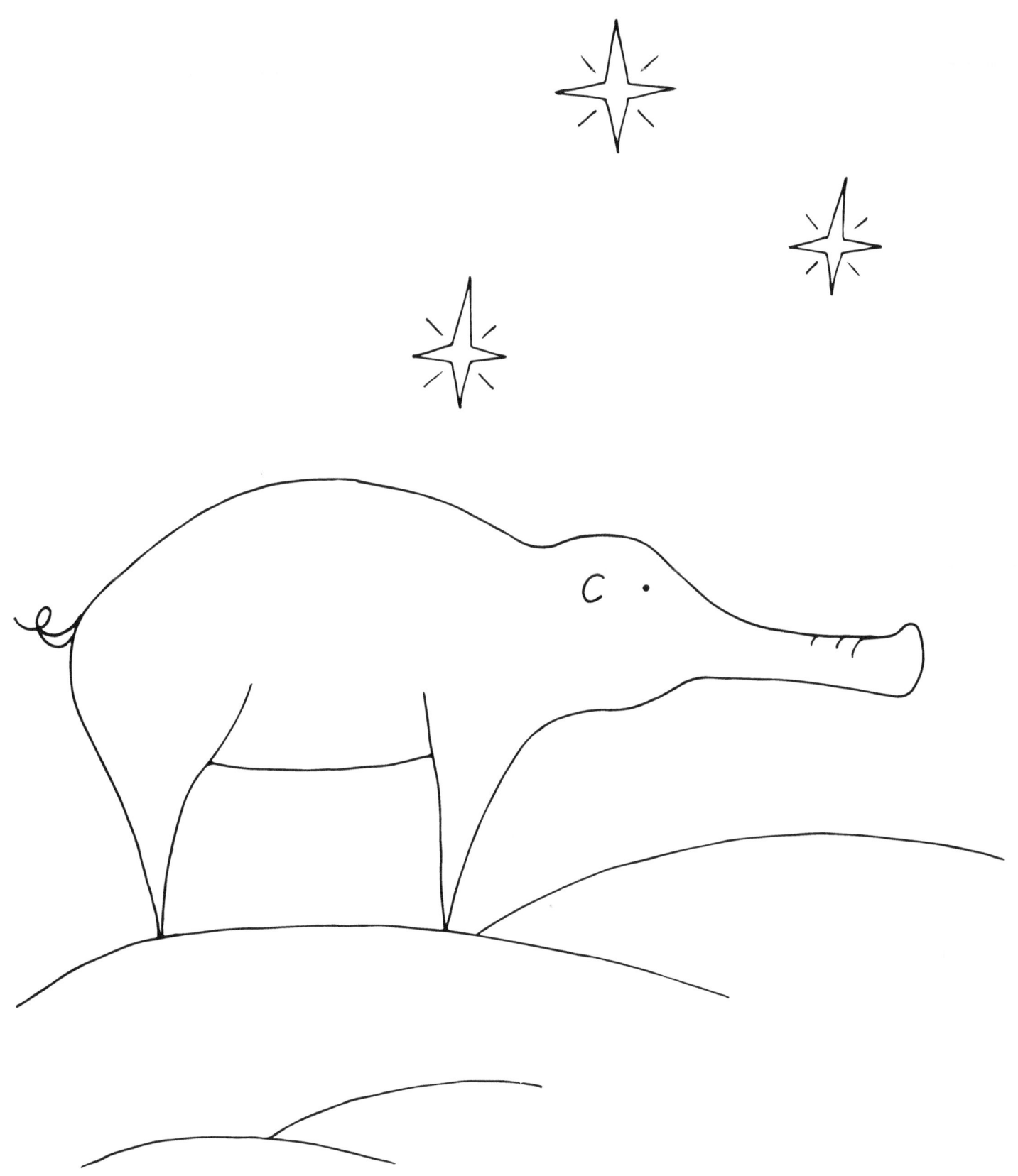

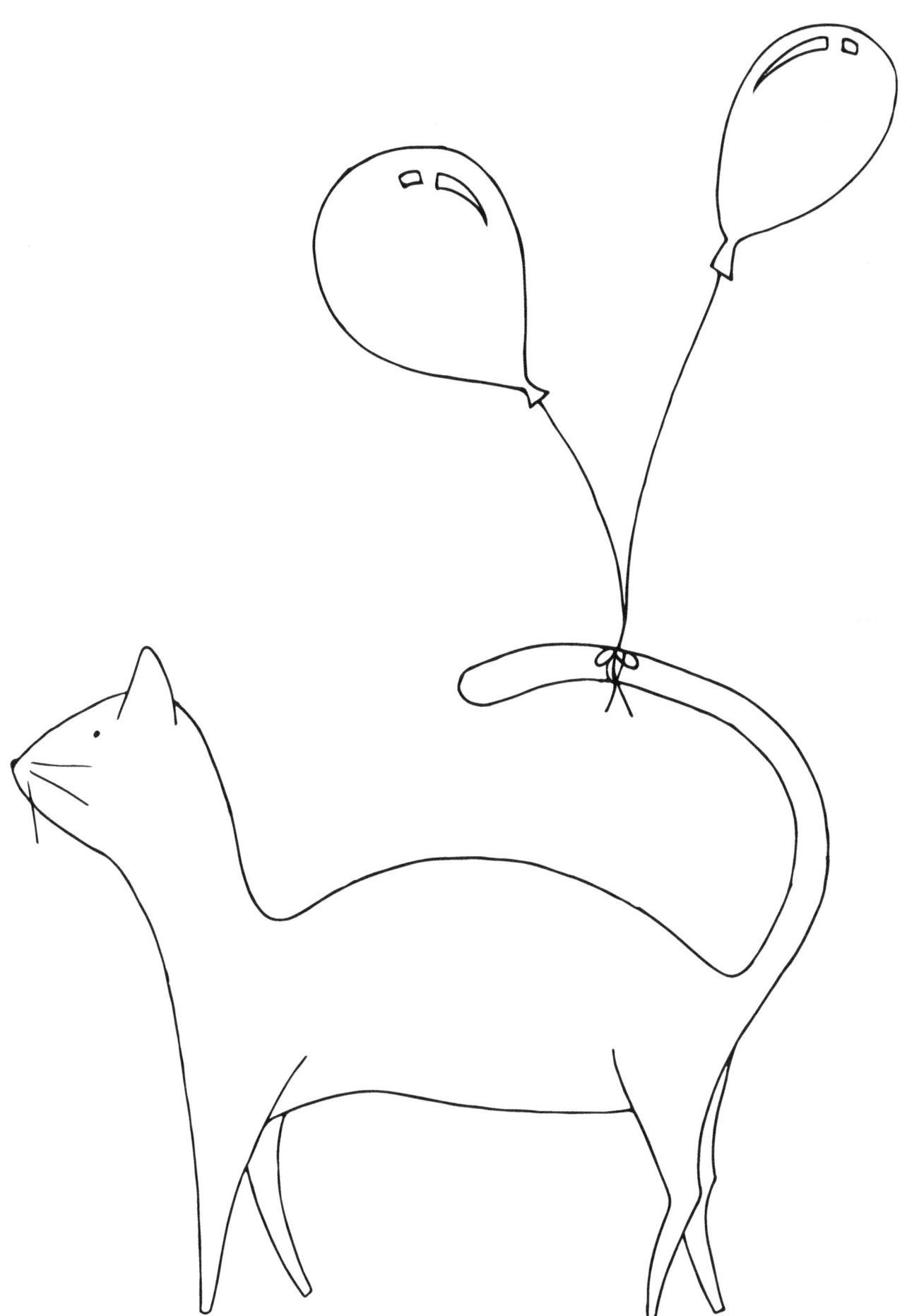

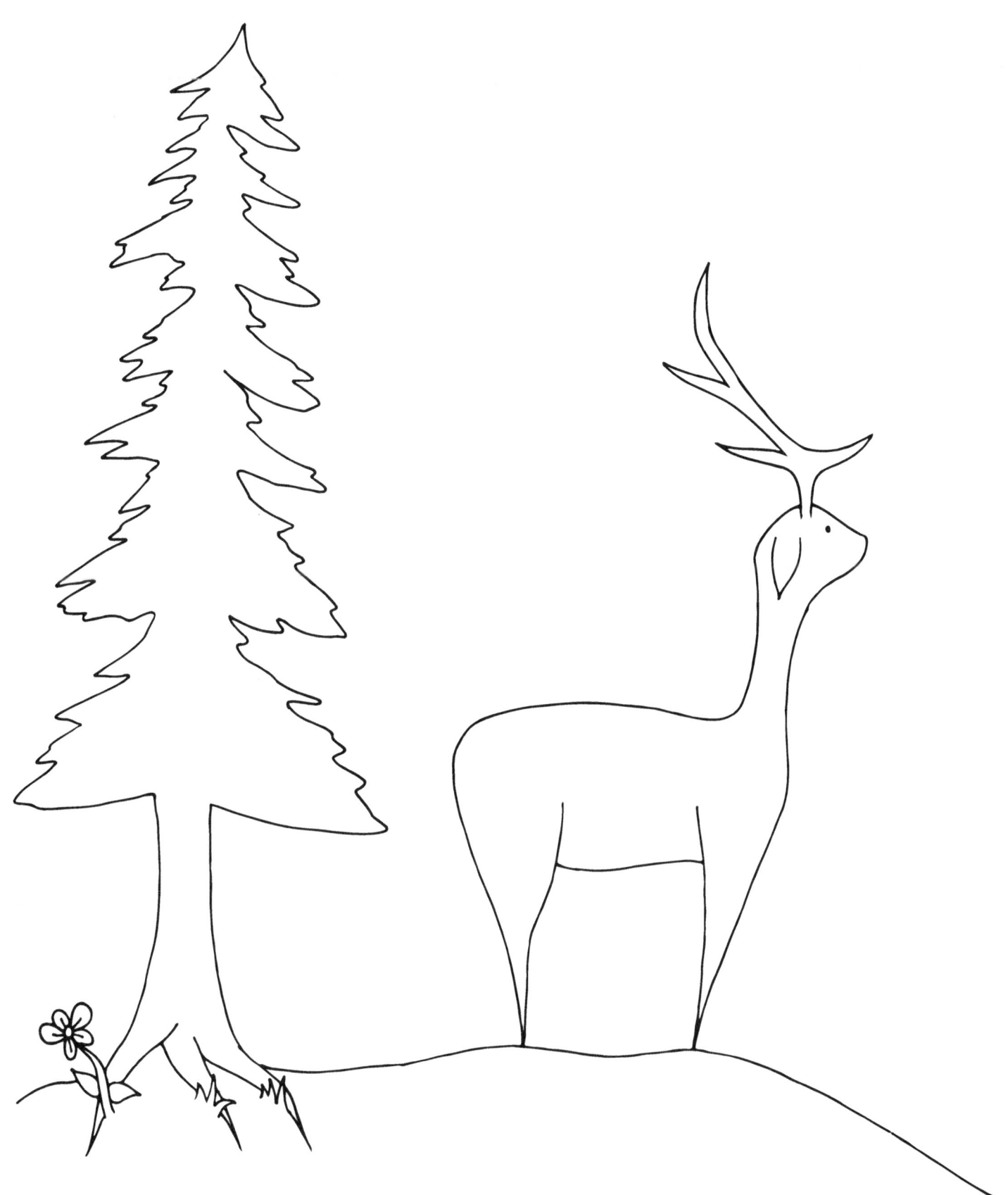

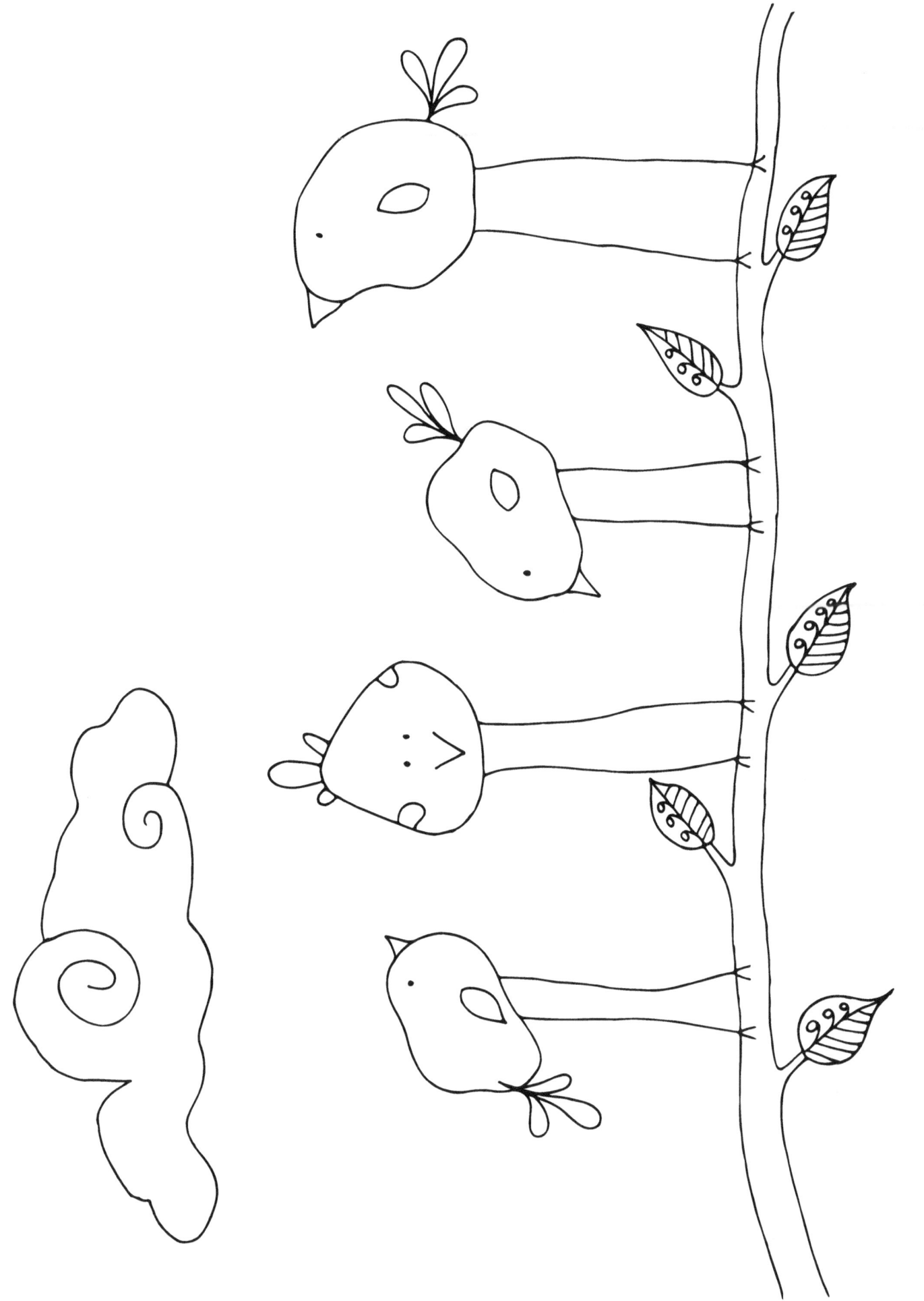

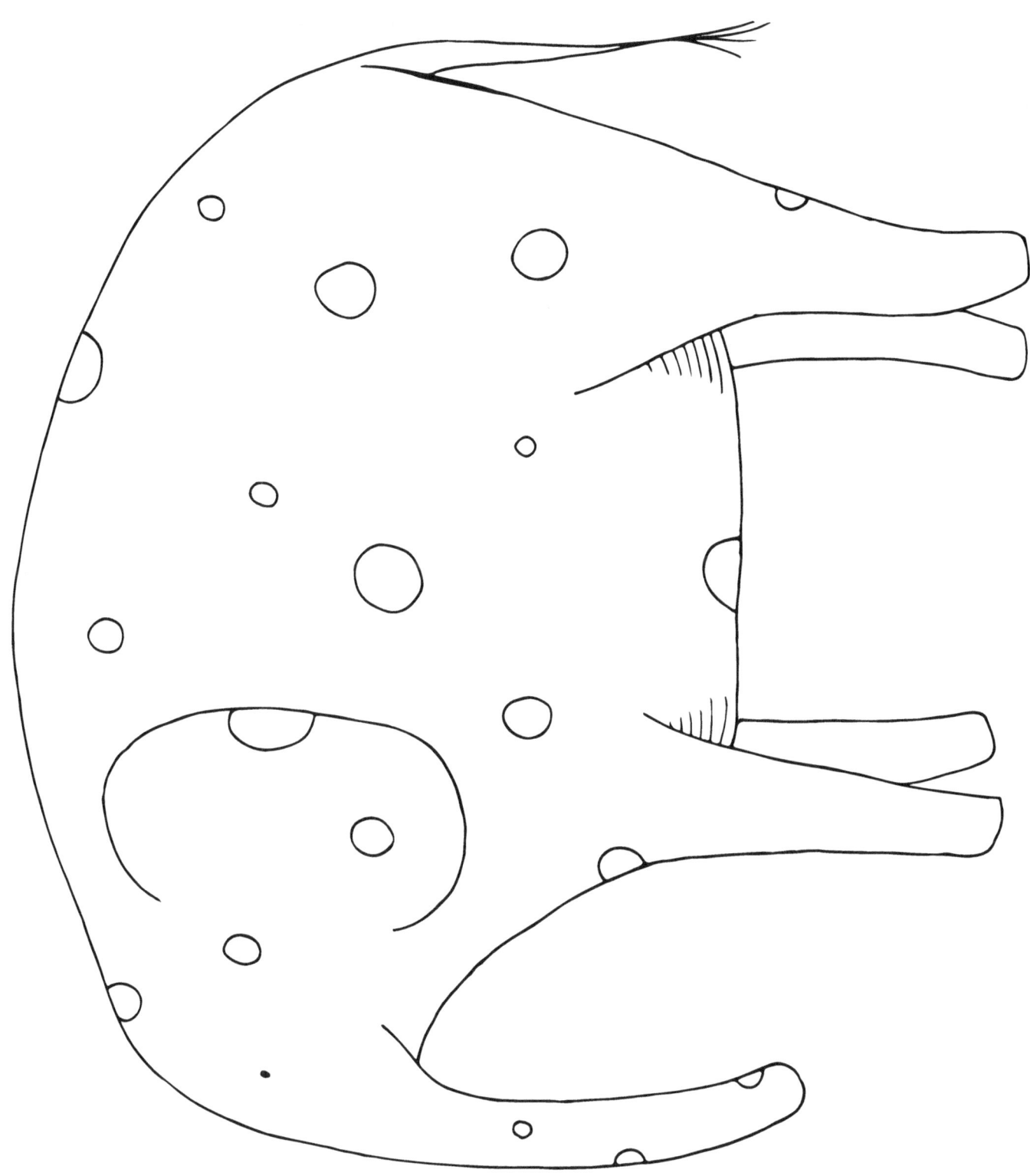

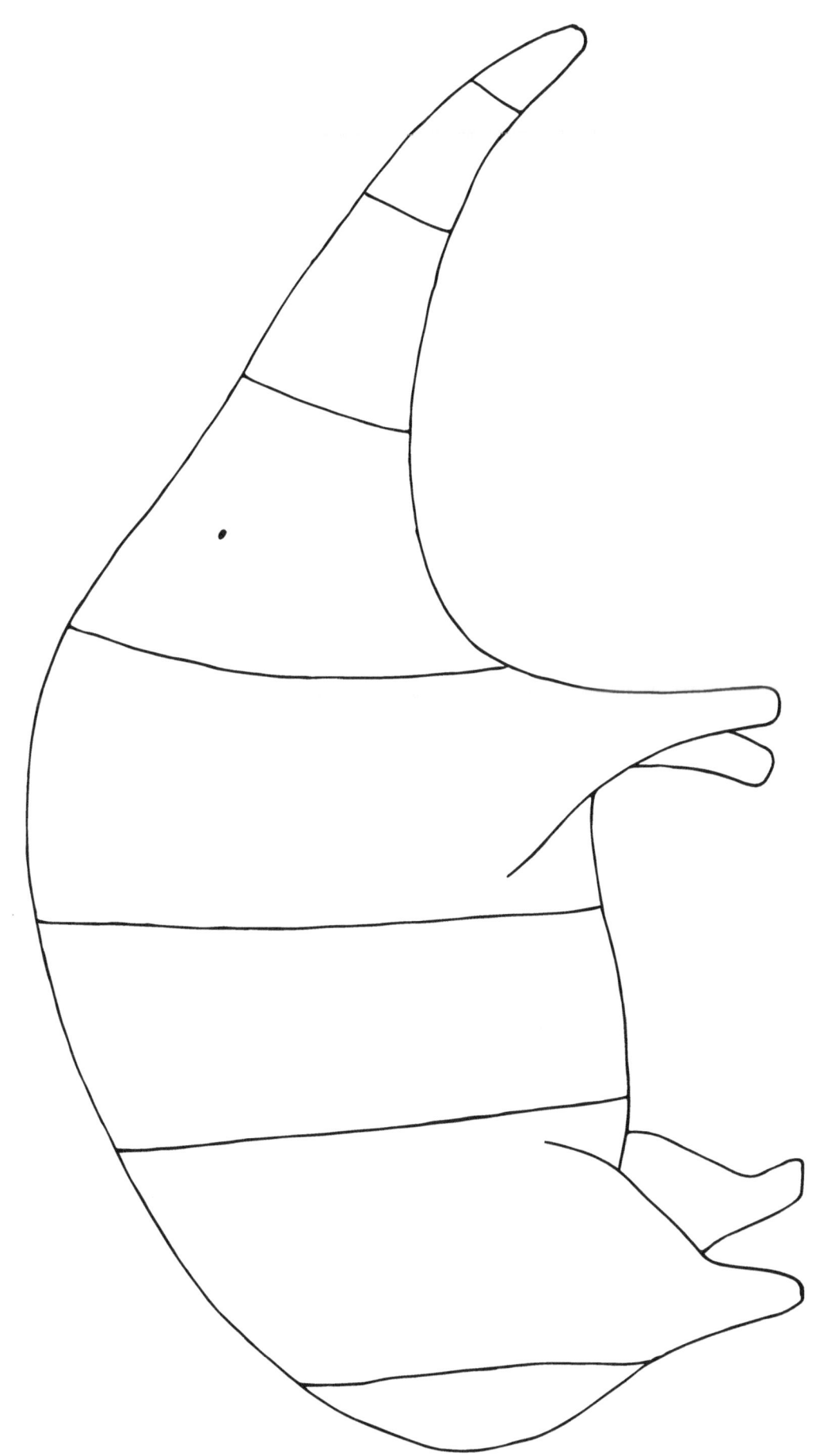

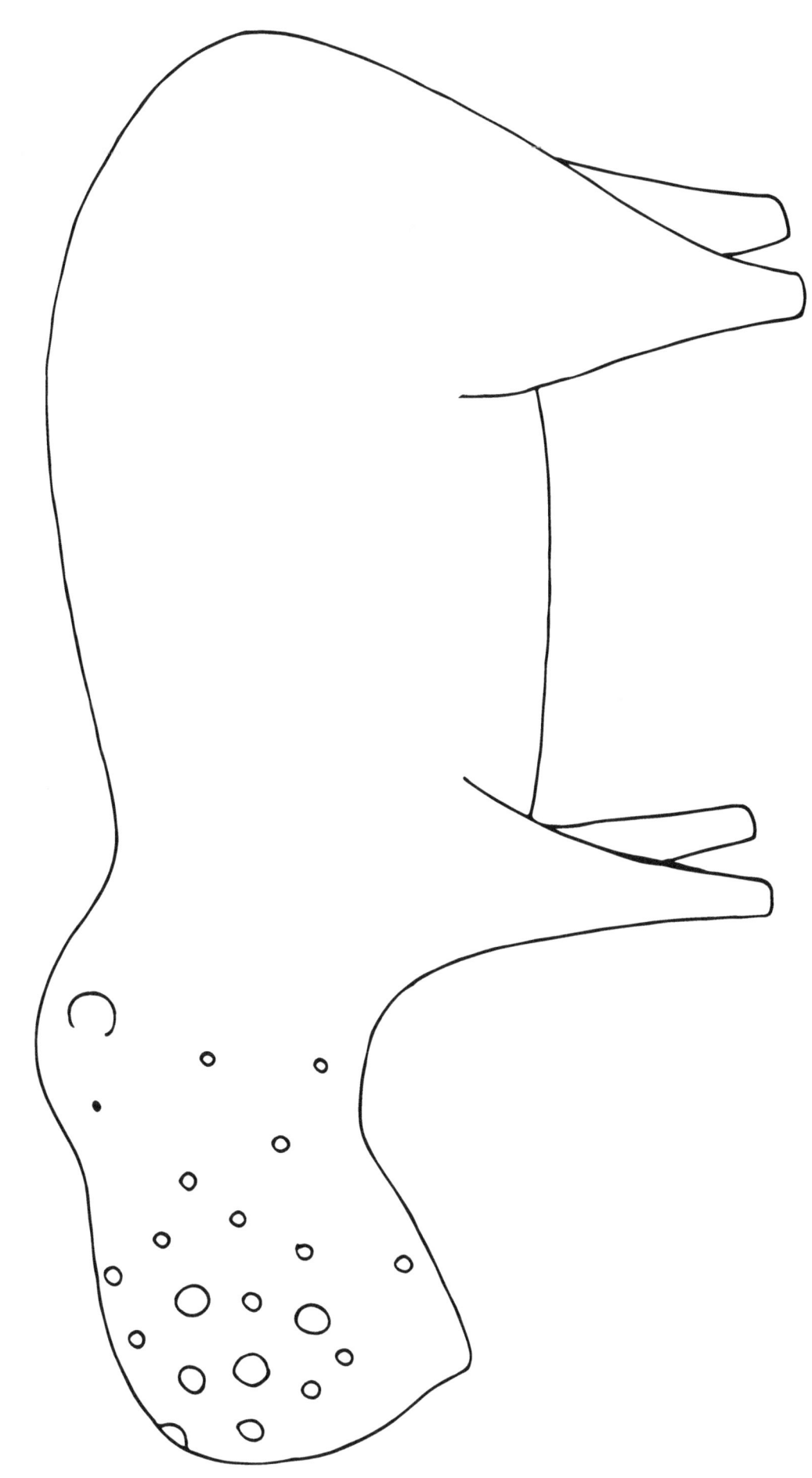

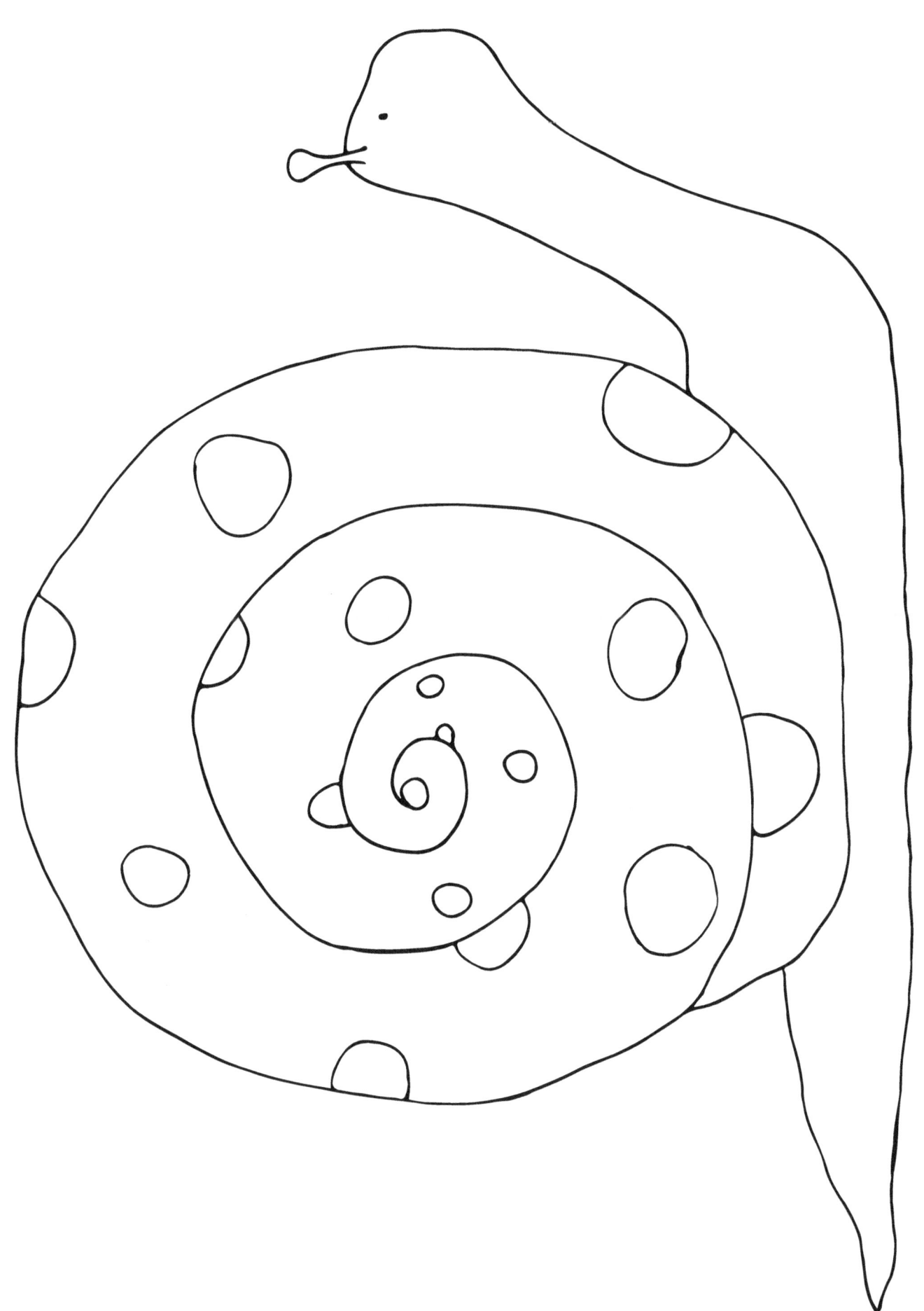

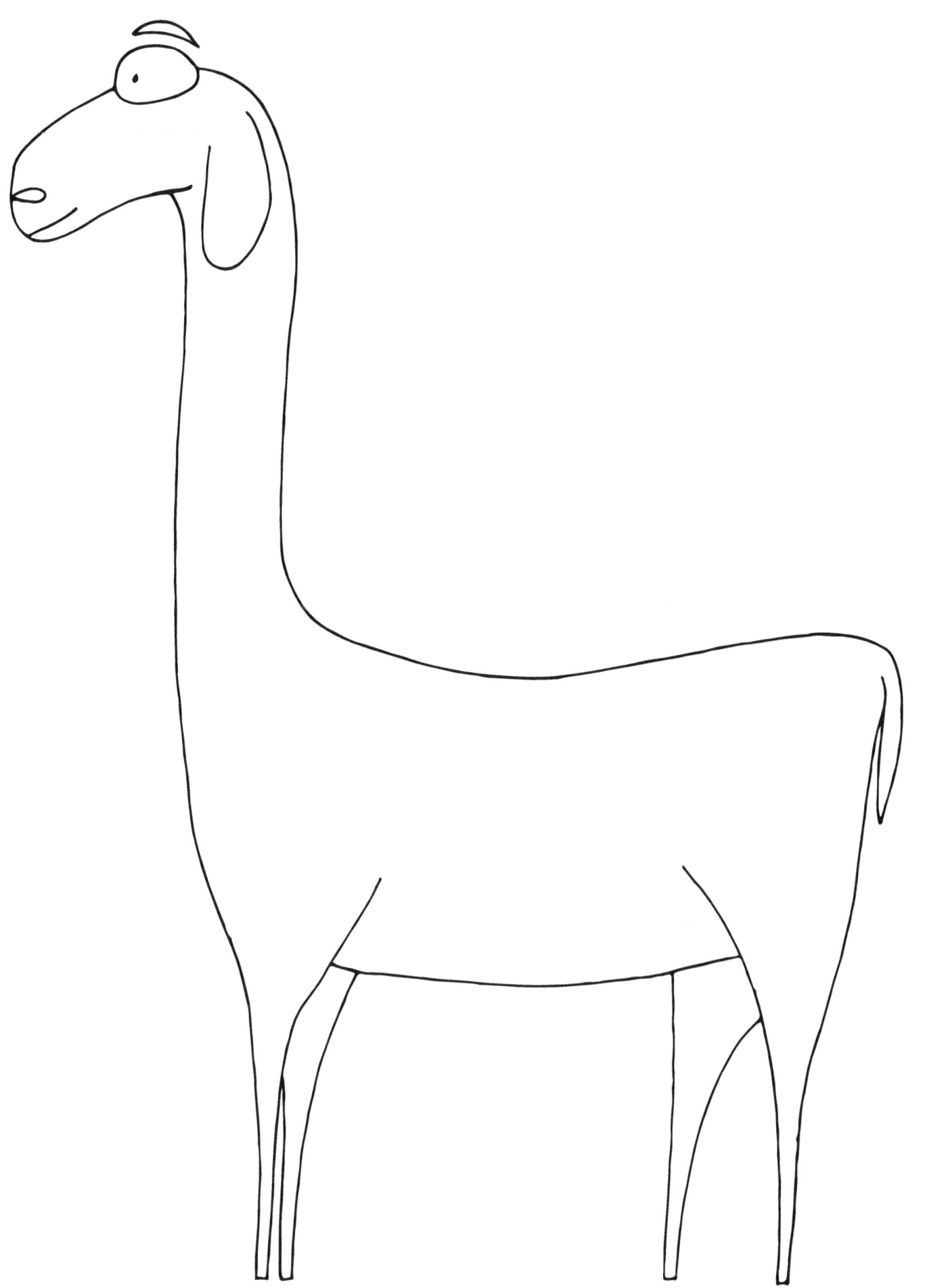

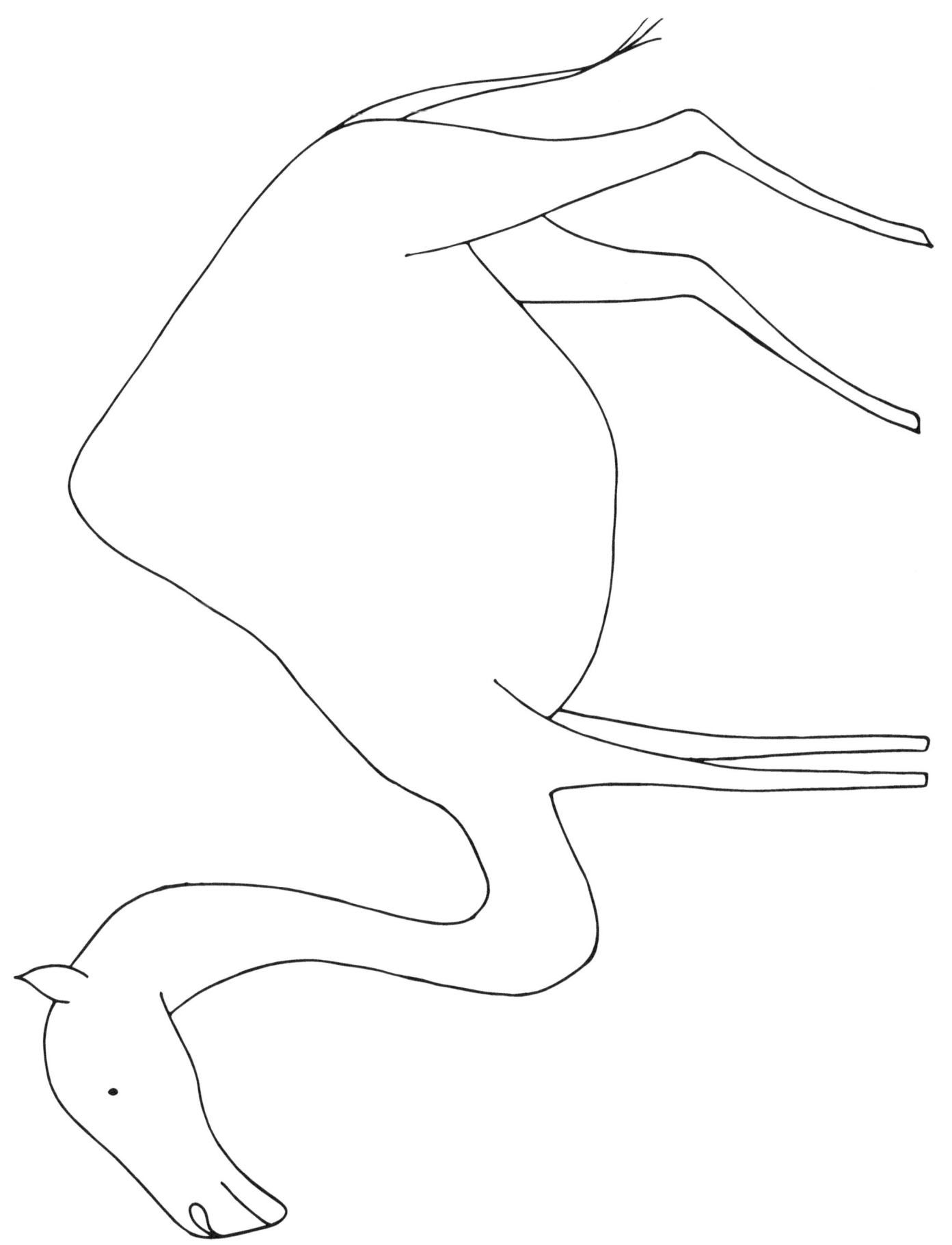

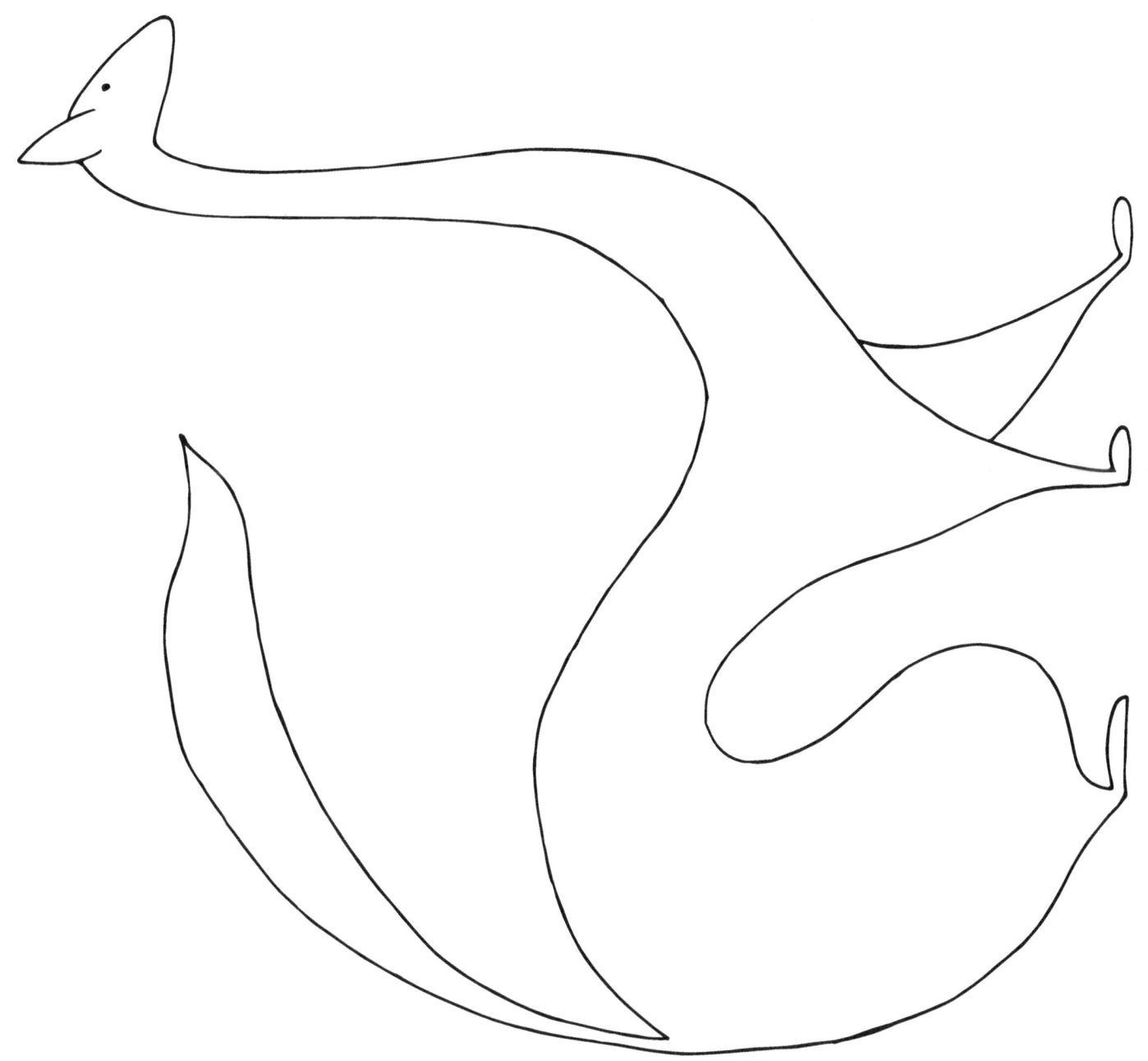

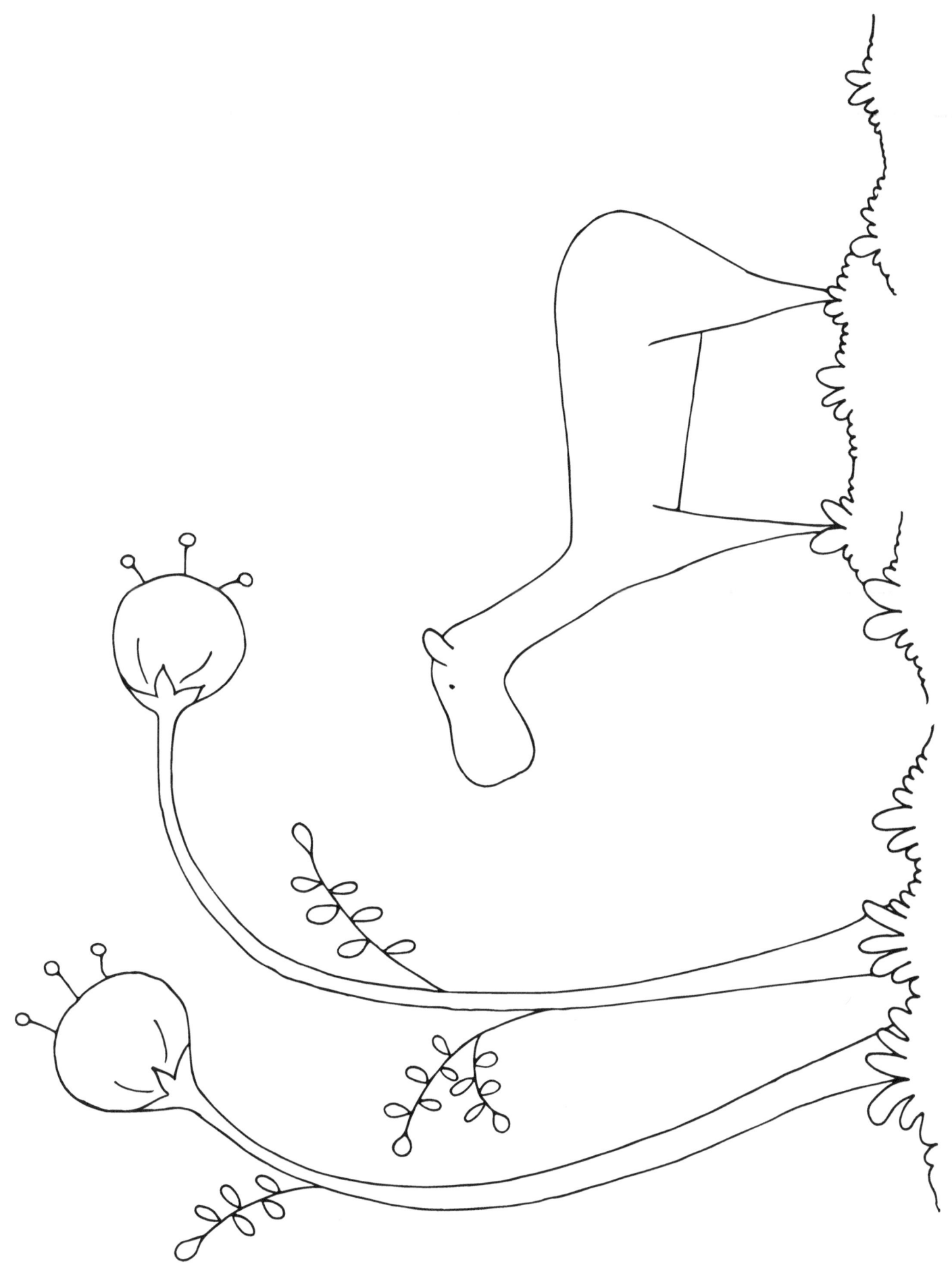

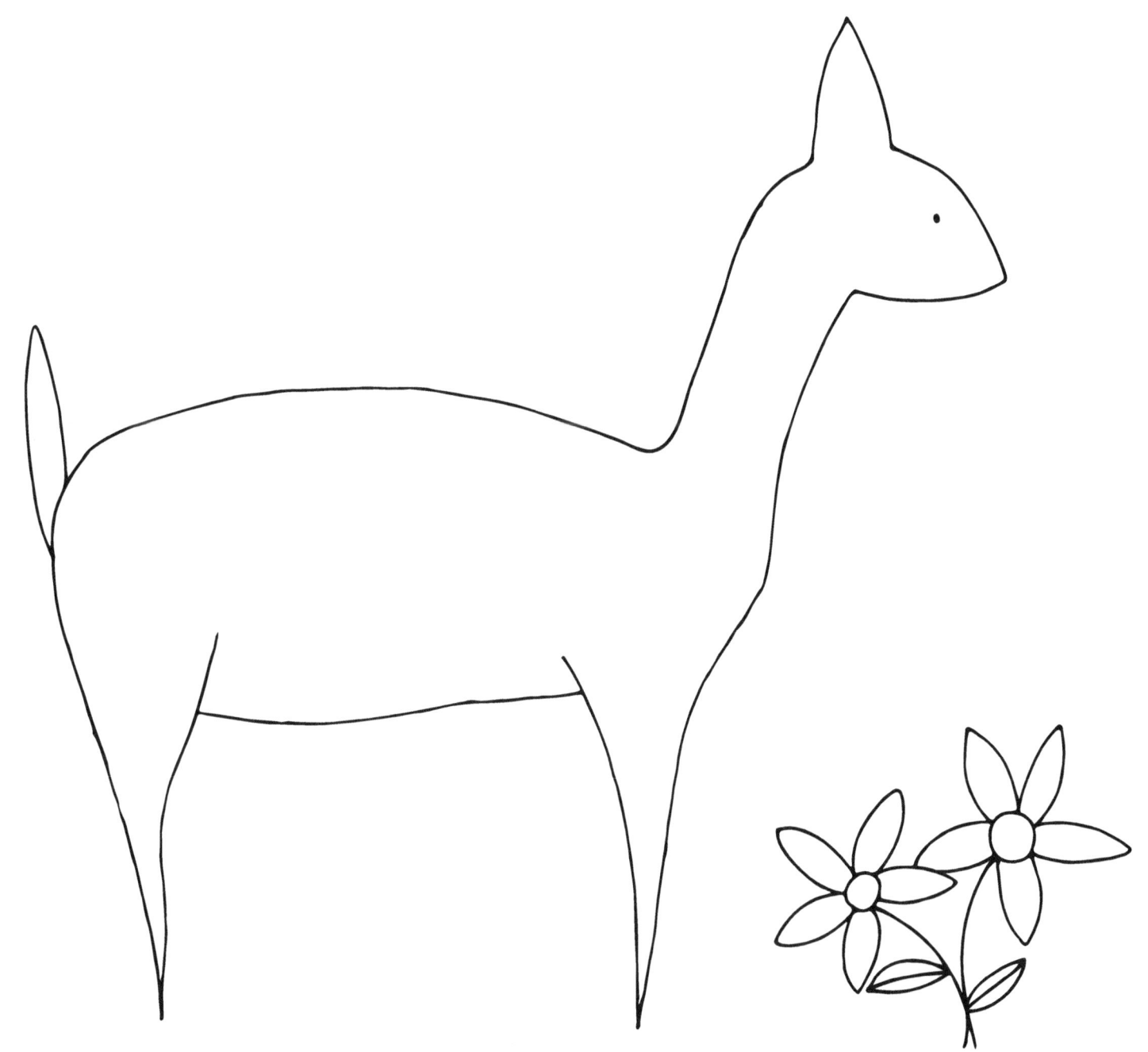

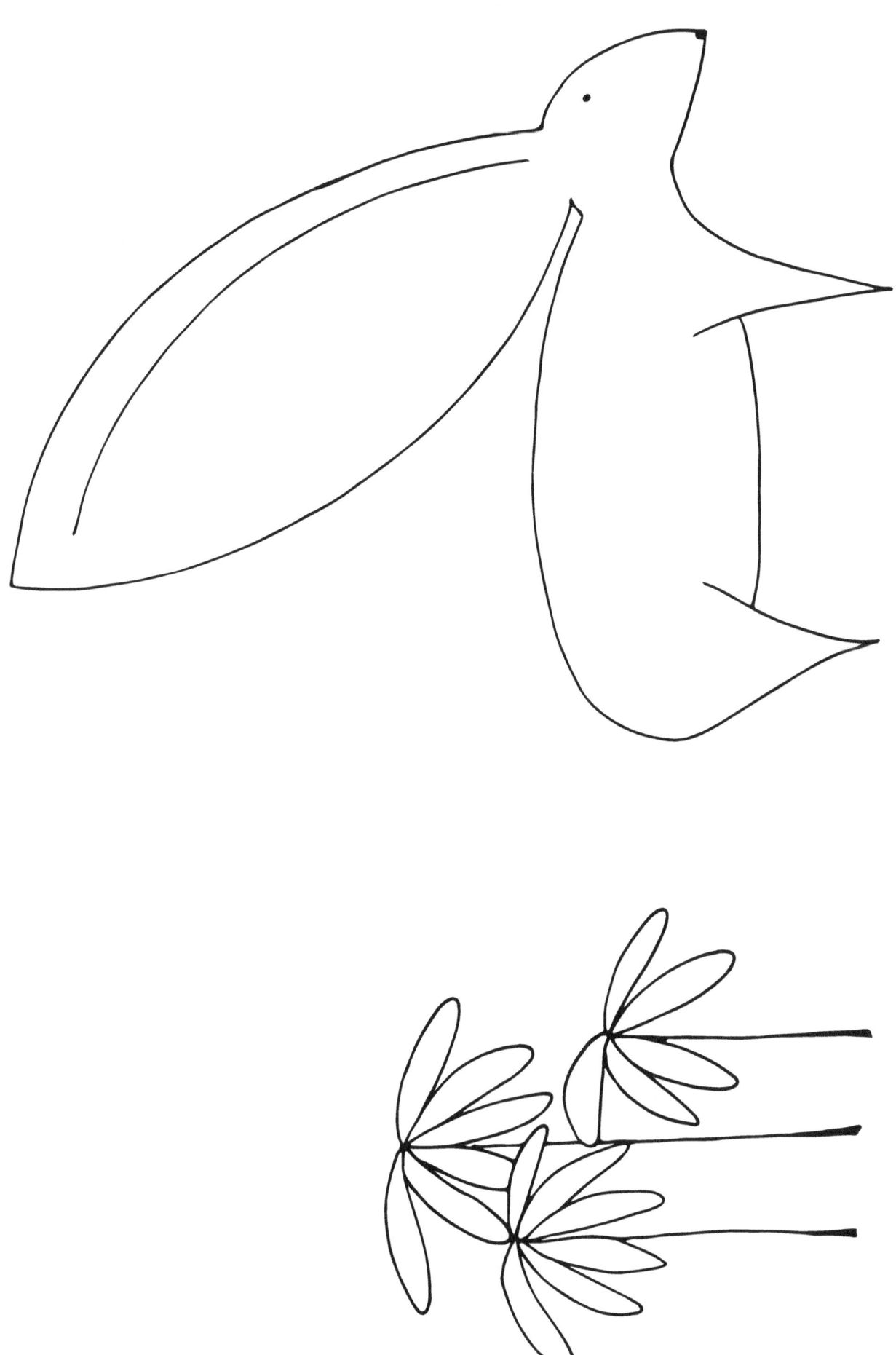

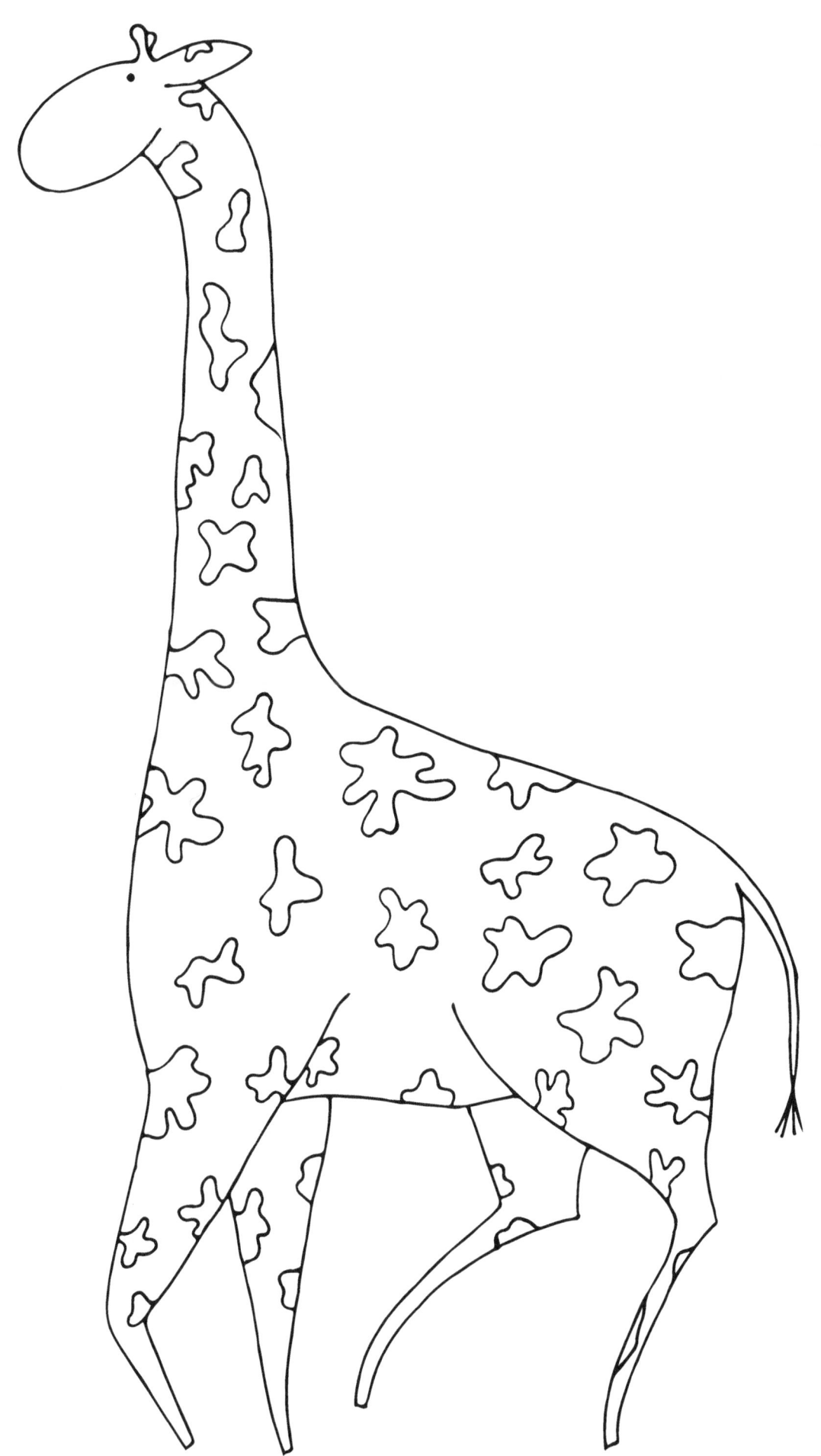

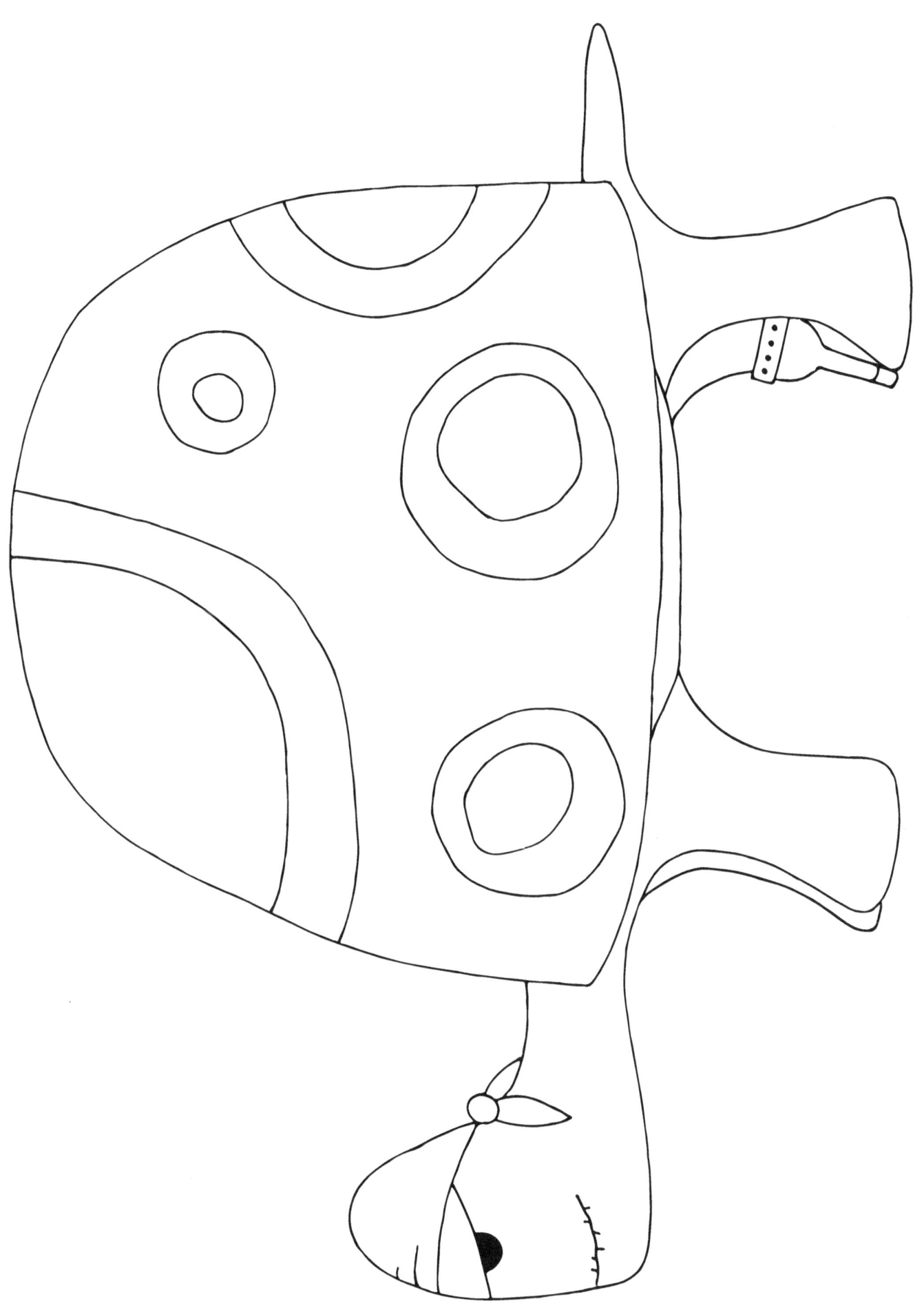

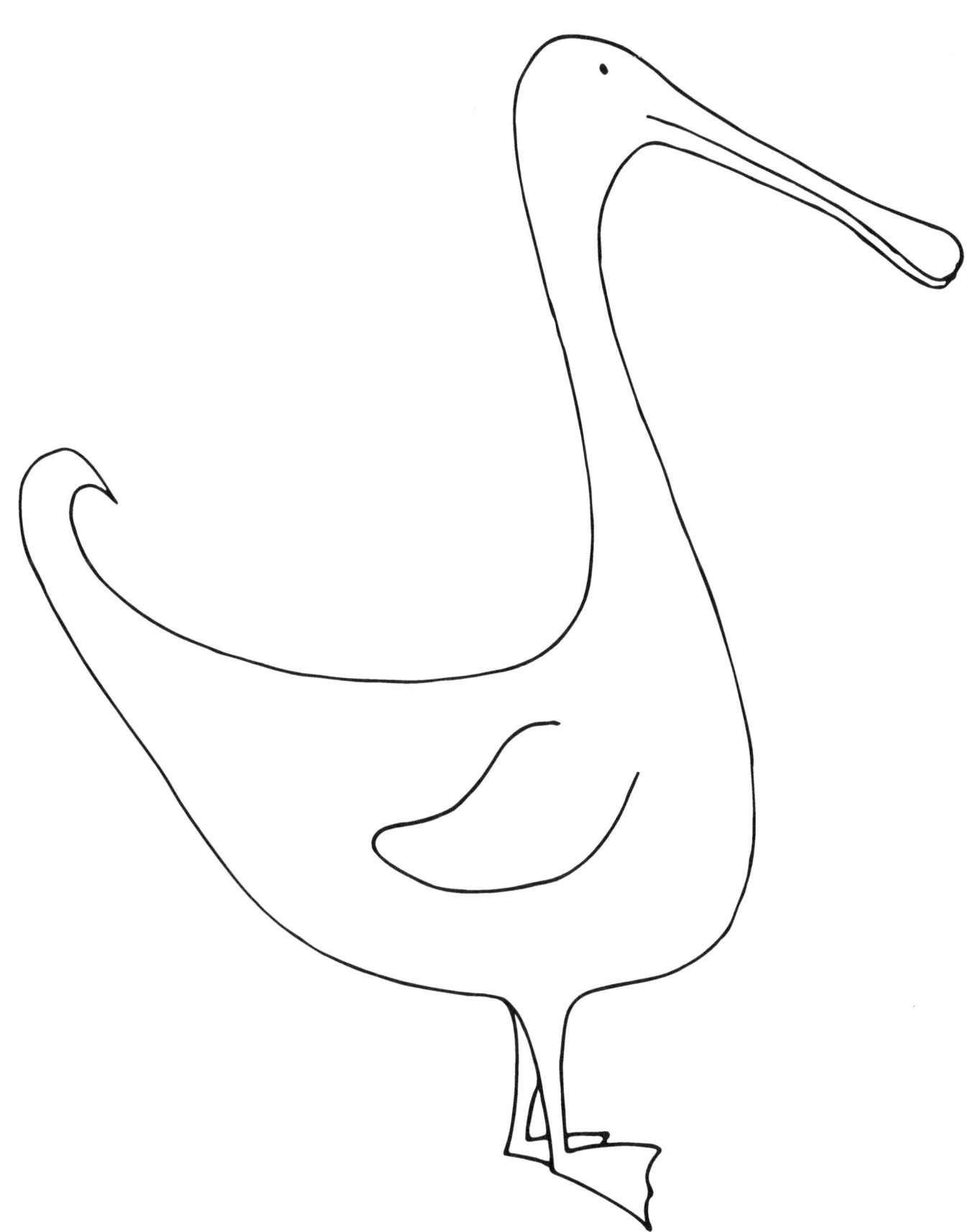

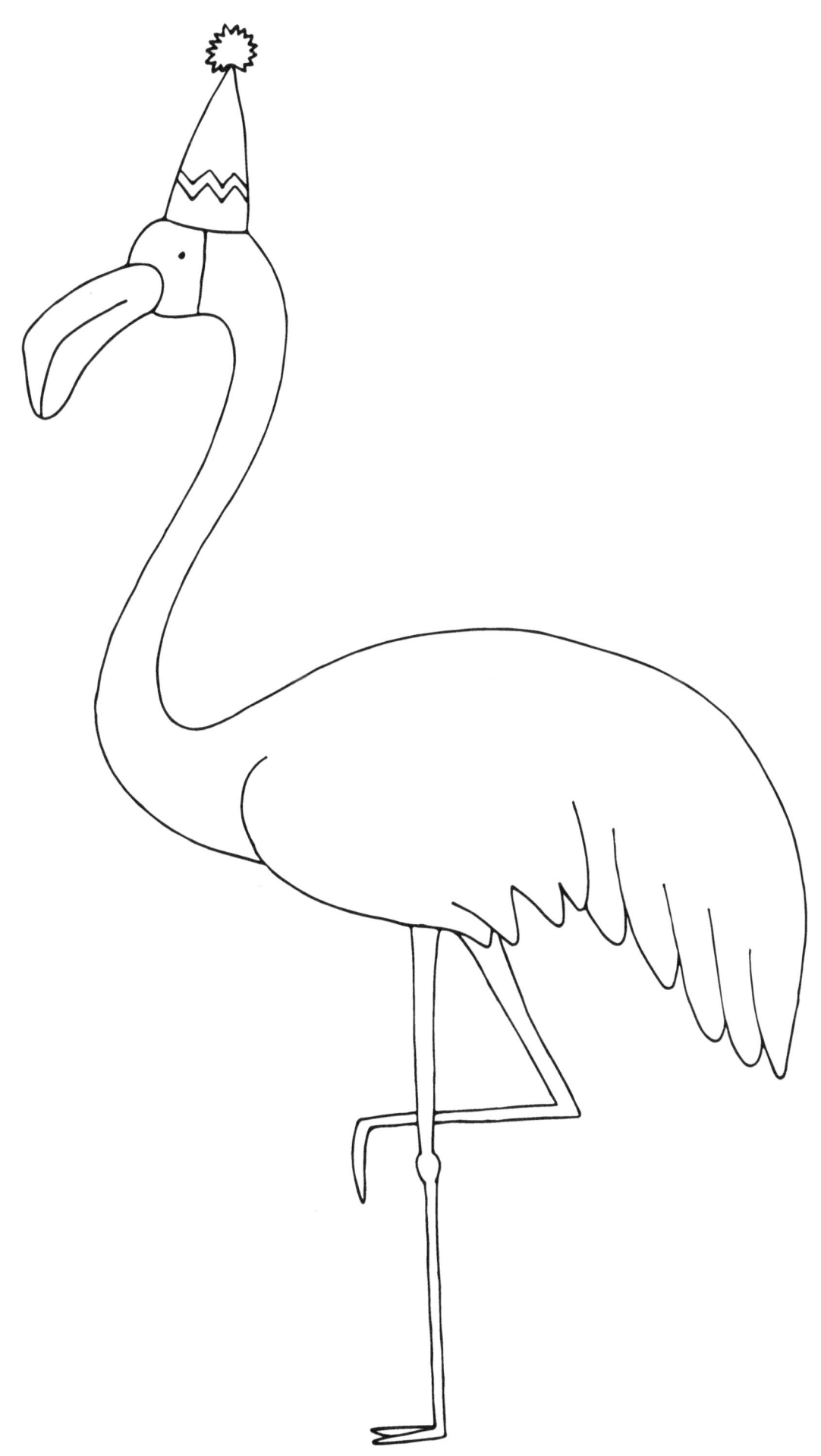

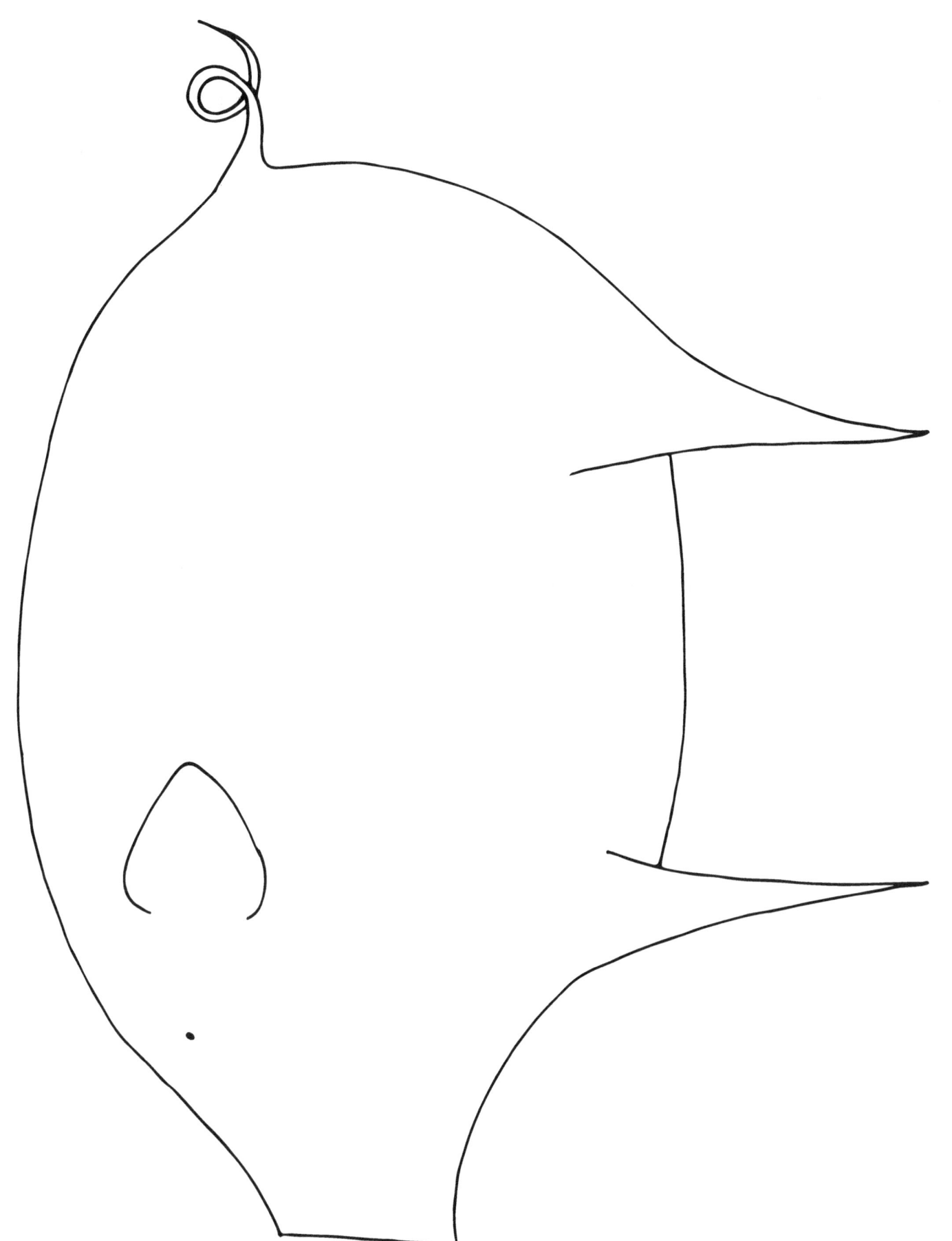

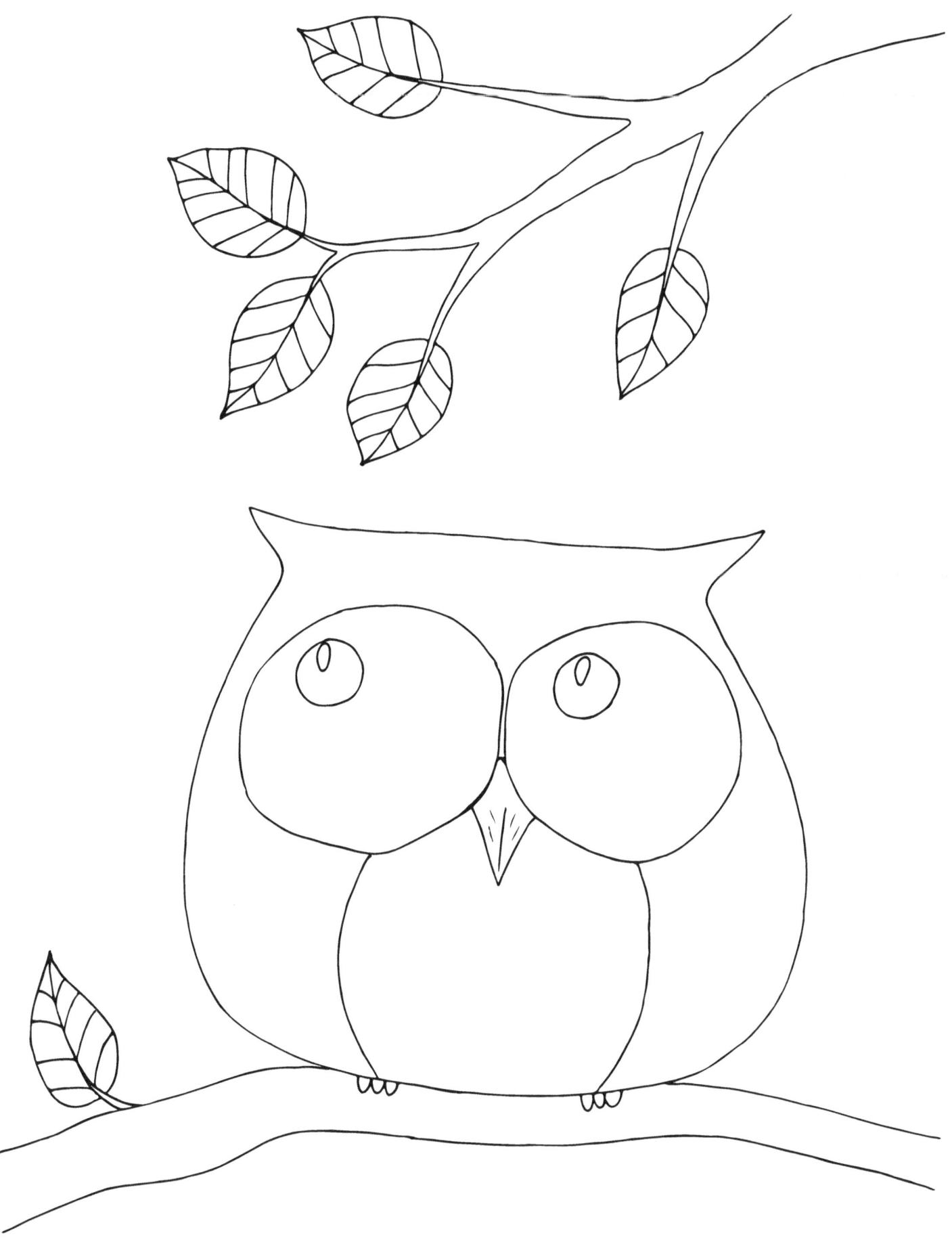

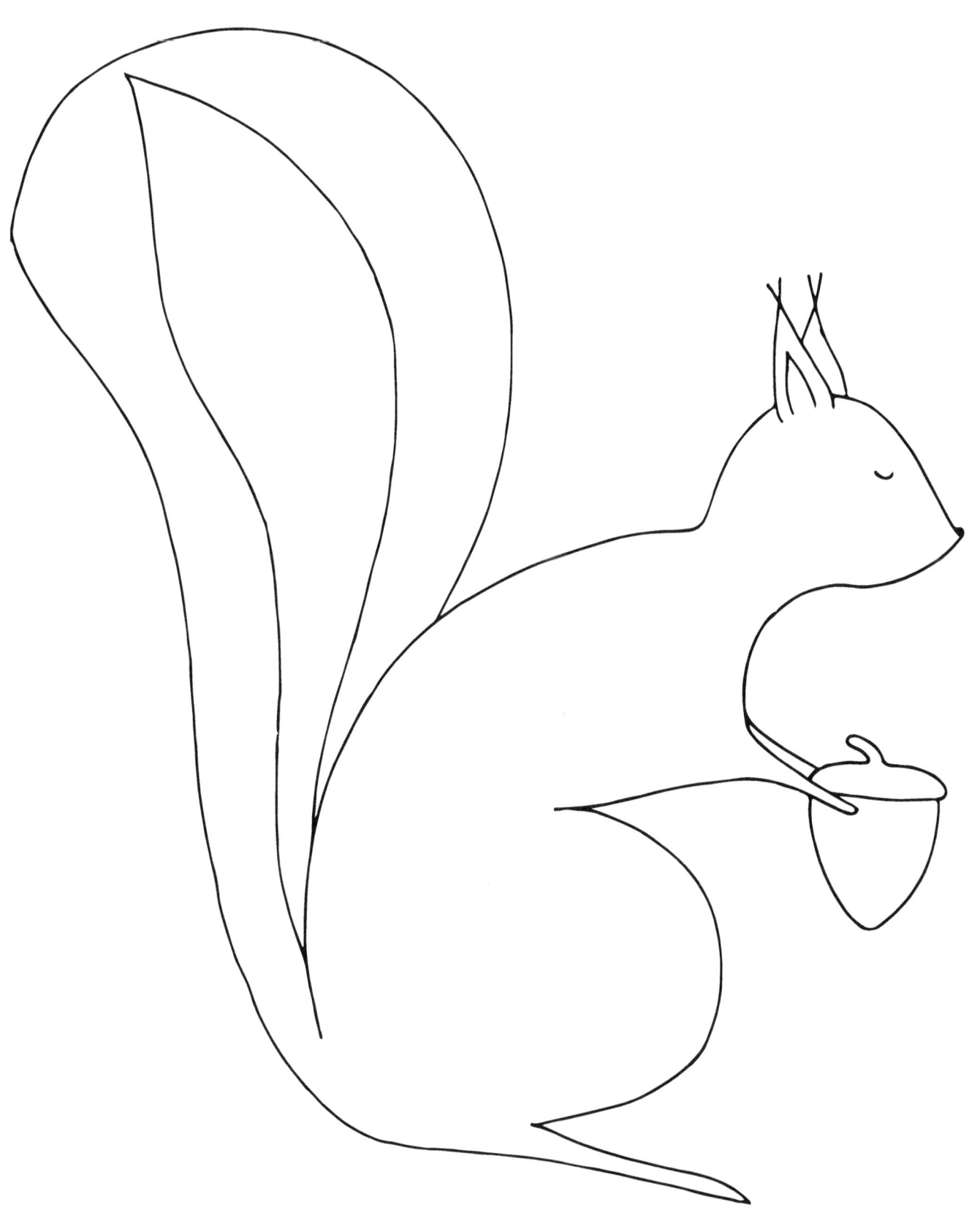

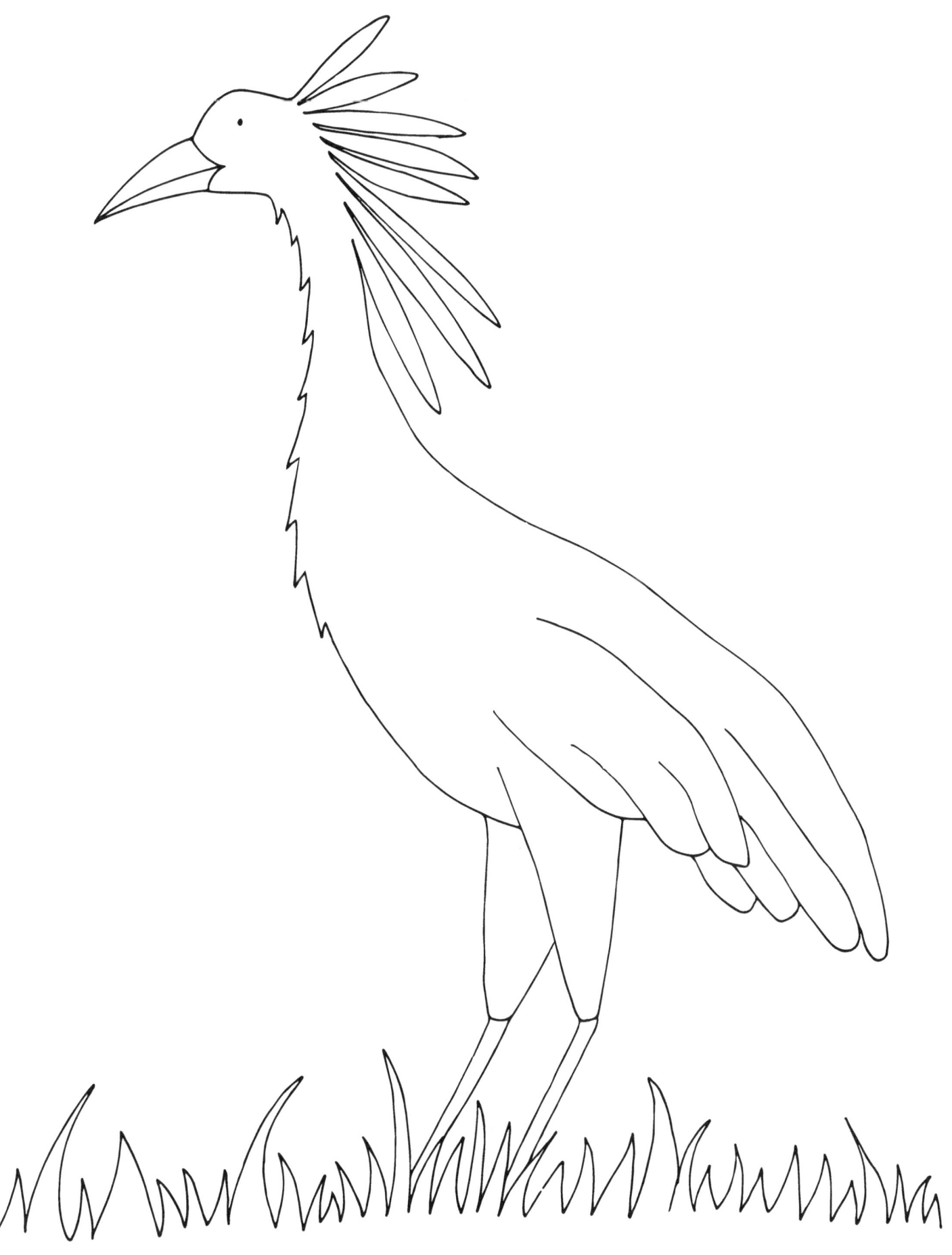

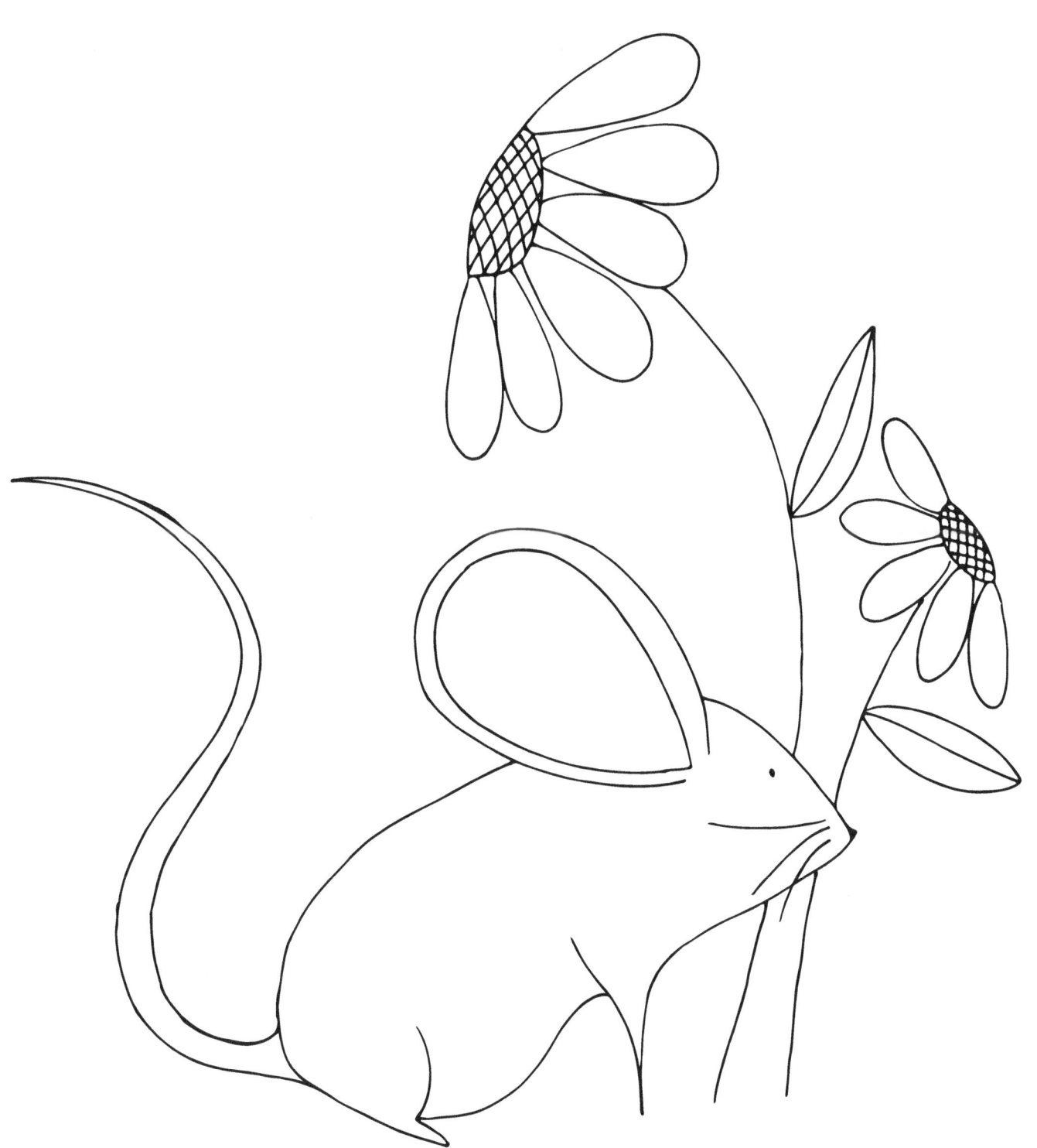

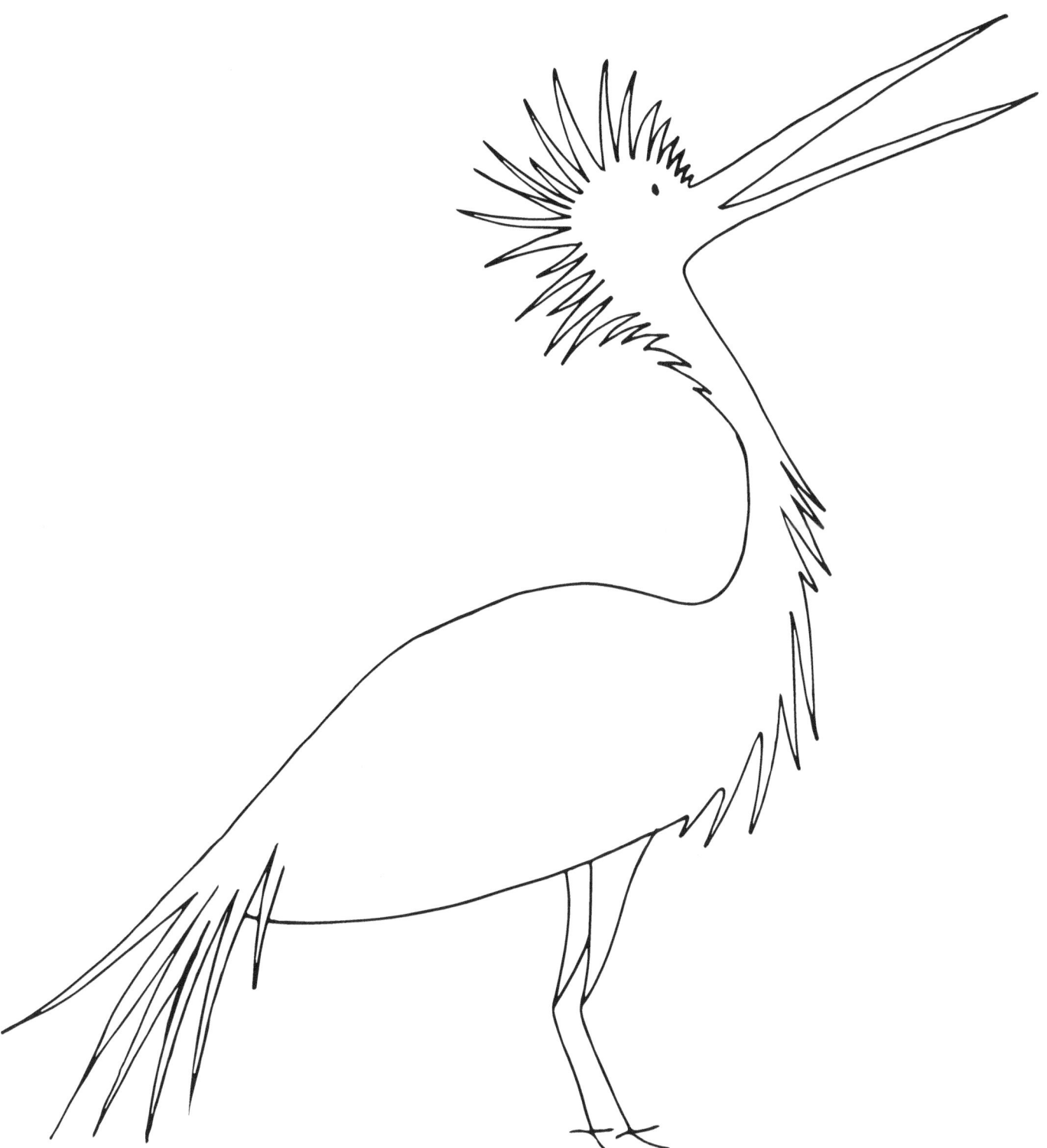

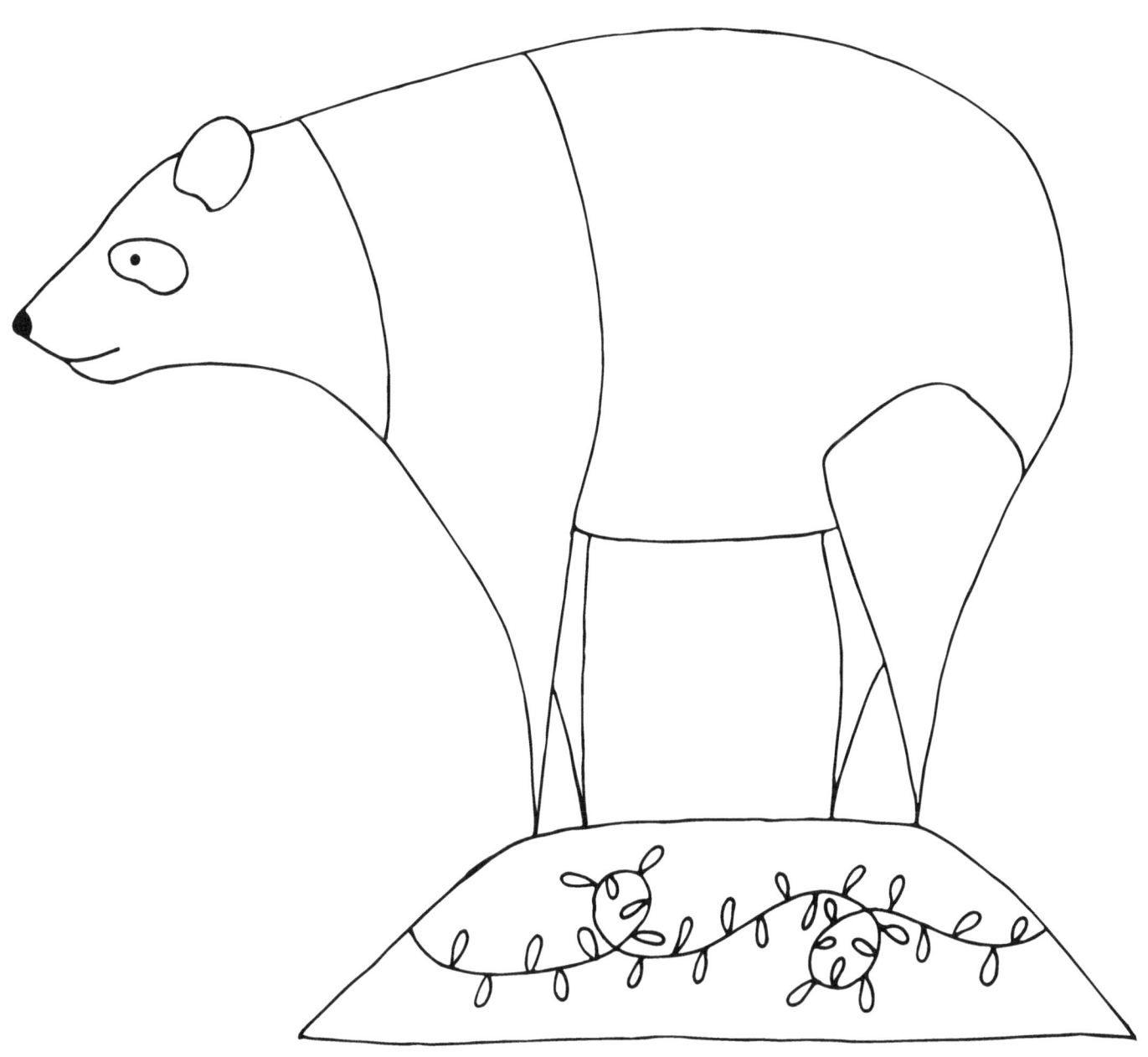

www.ingramcontent.com/pod-product-compliance
Lightning Source LLC
Chambersburg PA
CBHW080630190526
45169CB00009B/3344